The Spiralizer!
Cookbook

The Spiralizer!
Cookbook

the new way to low-calorie and low-carb eating: how-to techniques and 80 deliciously healthy recipes

the ultimate guide to the newest kitchen appliance for preparing vegetables and fruits, with over 450 step-by-step photographs

Catherine Atkinson

LORENZ BOOKS

CONTENTS

INTRODUCTION

The spiralizer is the newest tool in healthy eating – creating tasty low-carb, low-calorie noodles, ribbons and even 'rice' from everyday fruits and vegetables, all with the feel-full factor of real pasta.

So much has been written in the past decade about what we should and shouldn't eat that it's hard to know what dietary advice to follow, but one message has always been loud and clear; we should all eat more fruits and vegetables – they are the real superheroes of nutrition. Packed with vitamins and minerals, antioxidants and phytochemicals, they help keep the immune system strong and protect against a whole host of illnesses and diseases. While nutritionists are keen to promote 'eating five-a-day' (around 450g/1lb excluding potatoes) and more recently 'seven-a-day', most of us manage a measly three portions.

Spiralizers provide the perfect solution! Simply impale the produce between the spiked disc and slicing blade and turn the handle to make beautifully cut curly spaghetti-like noodles or concertina-like ribbons or slices in less than a minute. Vegetables are transformed, and preparing, cooking and eating them becomes easier and a lot more fun for you and the whole family.

The following pages offer a comprehensive guide to all the different types of equipment and their usage and assembly, all the techniques for spiralizing fruit and vegetables, and of course a fantastic collection of recipes to start you on your spiralizing journey.

Introducing spiralizers

If you are trying to shift a bit of weight or just to avoid gaining any, the noodles produced by a spiralizer make great guilt-free and low-carb alternatives to both pasta and potatoes. Try serving courgette (zucchini) noodles instead of spaghetti with bolognese sauce and you'll hardly notice the difference except in your health. You will have consumed far fewer calories and far more vitamins, minerals and fibre; a 75g/3oz cooked portion of spaghetti contains around 270 calories, compared with just 50 calories from noodles made from a large courgette – a massive bowlful. Make the swaps regularly and you will soon reap the benefits.

Eating more fruit and vegetables can have a number of positive effects. They are the best food sources of the antioxidants vitamin C and beta-carotene. These work to delay or even prevent oxidative damage to cells, which make you age more quickly and increase the risk of cancer and heart disease. They help to lower cholesterol and high blood pressure, raise immunity and prevent diabetes.

There's a strong link between what you eat and how you feel, whatever your lifestyle. Increasing your consumption of fruit and vegetables can do wonders for your skin, nails and hair. A good beauty regime can help us look good on the outside, but also needs to come from within, and a balanced diet is key here. Nutrients found in fruit and vegetables help rid the body of toxins and can counteract the effects of stress which eventually takes its toll on appearance.

WHAT CAN BE SPIRALIZED

A huge range of vegetables and some fruit can be spiralized into even-sized long and curly noodles, ribbons or slices. There are a few simple guidelines to checking which will be successful. The vegetable or fruit must be firm and solid, if it's soft or very juicy when gently squeezed it can't be spiralized. Vegetables must be fresh and when choosing produce such as pears, they should be just ripe and still very firm. The core shouldn't be either very tough or full of seeds. Immature seeds such as those in cucumber and courgettes are fine, but mature ones such as marrows (large zucchini) and those in the bulbous ends of butternut squash will jam the spiralizer. Small pips in apples and pears are not a problem and a horizontal spiralizer will remove these along with a section of the core.

For long noodles and spirals, the vegetable or fruit should have a diameter of at least 4cm/1½in (or you'll end up with crescent-shaped cuttings) and be at least 5cm/2in long, or there will be too much wastage.

BELOW: Spiralized vegetable noodles can make tasty and healthy main meals.

RIGHT: Colourful spiralized vegetables suit many different dietary needs and lifestyles.

SPIRALIZING FOR DIFFERENT DIETS

Spiralizing can be enjoyed by those who need or choose to follow restricted diets, not just for low-carb diets, but also gluten-free, low-sodium, high-fibre and paleo.

Gluten-free – In coeliac disease, the intestine cannot absorb food properly due to a reaction to gluten, a protein found in wheat, rye and barley, so starchy food like ordinary pasta must be avoided. Gluten sensitivity can start at any age and affects around one person in 130. It often runs in families and is more common in females than in males. Spiralized vegetables make a delicious alternative to all types of pasta; use fine vegetable noodles instead of spaghetti, medium noodles instead of linguine and thick noodles and ribbons rather than tagliatelle.

Low-sodium – Fruit and vegetables only contain minute amounts of sodium, so are ideal for those who need to watch their salt intake. In contrast the potassium content of many is high, which can help lower high blood pressure and reduce the risk of stroke and heart disease.

High-fibre – Fibre is essential for maintaining a healthy digestive system and is obtained solely from foods of plant origin. There are two types both of which are found in fruit and vegetables; soluble fibre binds cholesterol, so can help reduce the levels of cholesterol in your blood whereas insoluble fibre cannot be digested or absorbed by the body, so helps promote regular bowel movements. Fibre increases the feeling of fullness after a meal which may be beneficial for those who wish to lose weight as this will help to limit the amount of food eaten. Fibre also slows the rise of blood-sugar levels and helps improve the sensitivity of insulin which may lower the growing incidences of type II diabetes.

Paleo – The paleo diet is based on food eaten during the paleolithic era on the basis that our body's nutritional needs evolved at that time. Fans of the paleo diet aim to eat as naturally as possible and exclude dairy products, grains, legumes, processed oils and refined sugars from their diet, instead choosing grass-fed organic meat, wholefoods including nuts and seeds and an abundance of fresh fruit and vegetables.

KEY TO RECIPES

VT Vegetarian

V Vegan

GF Gluten-Free

DF Dairy-Free

P Paleo

Choosing and using a spiralizer

Like most kitchen gadgets, there are many different spiralizers to choose from and while all basically do the same job, choose carefully as some are more robustly build than others, or have features that you may desire or decide you don't want. It is worth checking out online reviews for the particular model you are interested in before you buy, as these often give an insight as to the reliability of the machine and other information such as whether it is relatively simple to get replacement blades. It will also let you know about any 'niggles' that current owners have. There are a few different kinds of spiralizer available and within these there is a range of sizes, shapes, colours and prices; it is these factors that you will need to think about before you decide which model is right for you.

USING A SPIRALIZER
Although there are several different types and many brands of spiralizer, they all work in much the same way. One end of the vegetable or fruit is held in place between a spiked holder attached to a turnable handle and an attachment (either a small metal ring or a spike) which holds it next to the noodle or slicing blade, so that when the handle is turned, noodles or fine slices are cut.

Most spiralizers come ready-assembled, so that all you need to do is remove it from the box, slot the required cutting blade in place, and start spiralizing. Others are usually simple to put together following the instructions provided. Before you begin, it's worth reading the manual or instruction leaflet which comes with your purchase, as well as the following pages which explain how to prepare individual types of fruit and vegetables before spiralizing. While some manuals are excellent, others, even on the most expensive spiralizers, are unhelpful or poorly translated. If you are unfortunate to have the latter, here are the basic steps for the different types of spiralizers you can buy.

ABOVE: A spiralizer with a slicing blade is an extremely useful tool; it can be used to create courgette (zucchini) ribbons.

Hand-held spiralizer

This is the very simplest and cheapest. Usually around 13cm/5in long and 7cm/3in in diameter, this has two built-in blades (one at each end) and is very much like a large pencil sharpener. The produce being cut fits into the cone shape and using one hand to hold the device, you then turn the vegetable or fruit into the cutting blade to produce either thin or slightly thicker vegetable noodles. Choose one which has finger guards to protect the user from the razor-sharp blades, and store in the box provided for safety.

Plus points: These are great for occasional use, or if you only have a small number of vegetables to prepare. It also allows you to spiralize produce directly into a pan or bowl. Washing up is minimal and a quick rinse under the tap will usually suffice, although most versions are supplied with their own little cleaning brush to deal with any bits of vegetable stuck in the blade and are also dishwasher-safe. The main advantage of this spiralizer is the relatively low price and its compact size; it will easily fit in a kitchen drawer which is useful if you have limited work or cupboard space.

Minus points: Blisteringly hard work if you are preparing large quantities or using for denser vegetables, such as carrots. It can also only be used for vegetables which have a diameter of 5cm/2in or less. After using, there will be a small piece of vegetable left unspiralized.

USING A HAND-HELD SPIRALIZER

This is the smallest and most basic model; you may find it a good choice if you intend preparing mostly softer vegetables such as courgettes and have very little kitchen storage space.

1 Prepare your choice of vegetable, following the guide on pages 20–51 (hand-held spiralizers are unsuitable for fruit such as apples or pears, but can be used for plantains); the maximum diameter of the vegetable should be no more than 5cm/2in.

2 Insert the vegetable into one of the cone-shaped ends of spiralizer (one end produces thin spaghetti-sized strands of vegetable, the other medium strands). Firmly push and twist the vegetable at the same time, over a plate or bowl to catch the strands.

3 Continue until the vegetable is about 2.5cm/1in longer than the cone, then place the spiked slicer cap on the end of the vegetable (this will protect your fingers from the sharp blades while you spiralize the last little piece).

4 Give the vegetables a few more twists until it can be turned no further, then lift up the cap and remove the remaining piece of vegetable attached to the spikes. Either discard or wrap in clear film or plastic wrap and keep for another recipe (see pages 52–53 for suggestions of how to use left-over pieces of vegetables).

Horizontal-hold spiralizer

These are the largest and probably the most popular spiralizers. They measure around 30 x 15cm/12 x 6in and usually come with three or sometimes four, interchangeable cutting blades. They cut anything from thin spaghetti-sized to wide tagliatelle-sized noodles. Most have a thin 2mm/1/12in noodle and medium 3mm/1/8in noodle cutting blade and a slicing blade. A few have an additional 4mm/1/6in (thick) noodle blade as well. The vegetable or fruit is placed in position between a spike and a metal ring and the handle is turned to create spiral strands or ribbons.

Plus points: Unlike a hand-held spiralizer, these can be used for larger vegetables and cope admirably with fruit such as apples and tough vegetables such as butternut squash and celeriac, although these take a lot more effort than tender vegetables such as courgettes (zucchini) and cucumbers. Most have a built-in storage compartment to store the blades neatly and safely, when not in use. Suction feet prevent the spiralizer from slipping when turning the handle.

Minus points: These take up more room than other spiralizer (although they are smaller than many kitchen gadgets). The metal ring cuts a core the size of a pencil from the centre of the fruit and vegetables which can be wasteful when preparing narrower vegetables, although is an advantage with fruit such as apples and pears as it removes most of the core. The blades are exposed, so care is needed when changing and cleaning them.

ABOVE: Some horizontal spiralizers have a 'pushing' handle which allows you to provide gentle pressure when spiralizing tougher vegetables. BELOW: Others have a skewer attachment for threading vegetable noodle spirals and curly fries.

Most horizontal spiralizers have three blades: one with rows of triangular metal cutters which produce spaghetti-sized noodles; one with two rows of slightly larger cutters which produces thicker, fatter noodles; and a third flat-edged slicing blade which will produce wide concertina-like ribbons or can be used to finely slice vegetables such as onions and cabbage.

USING A HORIZONTAL SPIRALIZER

Horizontal spiralizers are easy to use and usually come ready-assembled with interchangeable slot-in blades, two of which are stored in the machine when not in use.

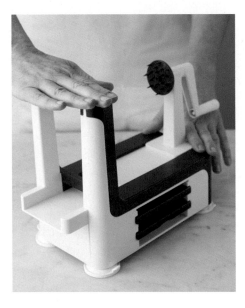

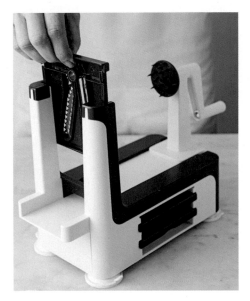

1 Prepare your choice of vegetable or fruit, following the guide on pages 20–51, making sure the cut ends are completely straight and flat.

2 Place the spiralizer on a smooth flat surface and press down firmly so that the suction rubber feet hold it securely in place.

3 Remove the desired blade attachment from the storage compartment and slide it into the holder, clicking it into position. Take care as the blades are very sharp.

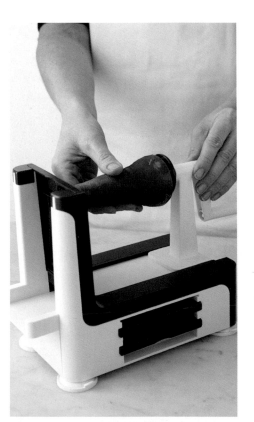

4 Position your fruit or vegetable firmly in place on the spiralizer. The wider end (if one is wider than the other) should be attached to the spiked crank and the narrower end pushed centrally against the blade holding ring.

5 Place a plate or shallow bowl under the blade to catch the spiralized produce, then turn the crank handle in a clockwise direction without stopping, applying gentle pressure, if needed, until the vegetable is spiralized. There will be a thin pencil-sized core and an end piece of vegetable, which you can discard (see pages 52–53 for ways to use).

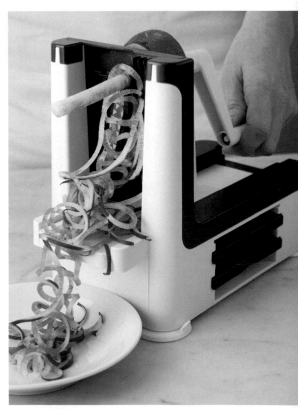

13

Vertical-hold spiralizer

This is a medium-sized upright gadget. The vegetable is placed on top of the blade, so pressure is exerted downwards as you turn the handle. Because the vegetable is held vertically, there is no need for a metal ring on the blades to hold the produce in place; this means that the core isn't cut out, so virtually the whole fruit or vegetable is used (if this is a feature you particularly like, do check before buying as a few vertical-hold spiralizers do remove the central core). The most expensive types sit securely on the work surface with suction feet and have high-quality comb-like blades, the smallest of which are just 1mm/$\frac{1}{32}$in and produce fine angel-hair or vermicelli-like strands.

Plus points: They are more compact than a horizontal-hold spiralizer. Some have a wider range of blades for producing very fine spiralized vegetables; with others, you can cut directly into the storage container, which is particularly handy for slicing vegetables such as tear-inducing onions. There is much less wastage as the core of the vegetable isn't removed.

Minus points: Not so great for fruit such as apples and pears as the core isn't removed when spiralizing. While the blades in some can be changed simply by turning a switch on the side of the spiralizer rather than manually, others have exposed blades which are slightly more fiddly to slot into position and many versions have no storage facility for the blades. Because the spiralized noodles or slices drop on to the surface below the machine, you will need to stop occasionally to remove the noodles as you work or you may find the juices spreading on the work surface. It is also vital to keep the feet of the spiralizer extra-clean as the noodles will come into contact with these.

ABOVE: Vertical-hold spiralizers are useful for cutting tricky vegetables, such as onions, into thin strands.

BELOW RIGHT and BELOW: Some vertical-hold spiralizers have blades set in a plastic casing; others have loose comb-like blades, which should be stored in a small container for safety.

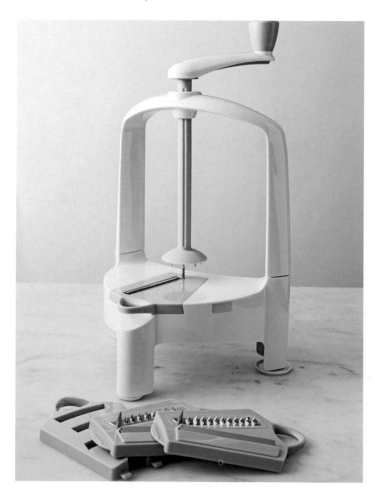

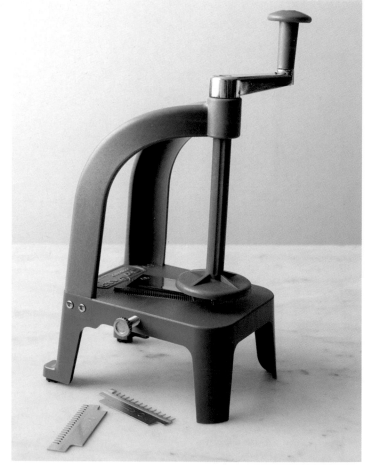

USING A VERTICAL SPIRALIZER

Place your vertical spiralizer on a large board or a scrupulously clean work surface as the noodles or slices fall directly on to the surface below.

1 Place the spiralizer on a smooth flat surface. If it has suction feet, press down firmly, so that these attach to the surface and hold the spiralizer in place.

2 Slot the required blade into place, making sure it is the right way round, or it won't cut, then secure by twisting and tightening the holding screw.

3 Prepare your choice of vegetable or fruit, following the guide on pages 20–51.

5 Turn the crank handle in a clockwise direction, until the vegetable is spiralized. Stop every now and then and remove the noodles, transferring to a bowl or plate. Continue until the vegetable is spiralized and the handle will no longer turn; there will be a small piece, about 1cm/½in left at the end, which you can discard (see pages 52–53 for ways to use).

4 Place upright on to the metal spike, making sure that you position it centrally. Lower the winder spike, so that it presses down on the top end of the vegetable, holding it securely.

Enclosed spiralizer

These work in much the same way as vertical-hold spiralizers but have a large removable integrated container to catch the prepared noodles or slices. Designs vary considerably and some have slot-in blades encased in plastic, others have built-in blades on a square pivot which are changed by turning a knob on the side of the spiralizer. They may have rubber suction feet to firmly attach to the work surface or be hand-held and portable. Some are multi-task appliances and come with additional attachments for juicing and grating.

Plus points: The main advantage of these is that prepared noodles fall straight into a container, so there is much less mess and no need for a separate plate or bowl to catch the noodles. The container can be used for storage, although a lid isn't provided, so you will need to cover with clear film or plastic wrap (avoid storing beetroot or carrot noodles which might stain the container if left for too long). Some are lightweight and portable and can be used without the container, spiralizing directly into a mixing or serving bowl, or a pan. Usually compact machines, enclosed spiralizers tend to take up less work surface or cupboard space than horizontal-hold spiralizers. Those with enclosed blades are safer to use.

Minus points: Container space is limited, so you may have to remove and transfer noodles if you are preparing larger amounts of vegetables. In some, the limited gap between the attachment spike and blades means that vegetables have to be cut into shorter lengths, so there will be more wastage.

ABOVE: Great results can be achieved with an enclosed spiralizer, with much less mess than other gadgets.

BELOW LEFT and RIGHT: Some enclosed spiralizers can be firmly attached to the work surface with rubber suction pads; others are lighter to carry.

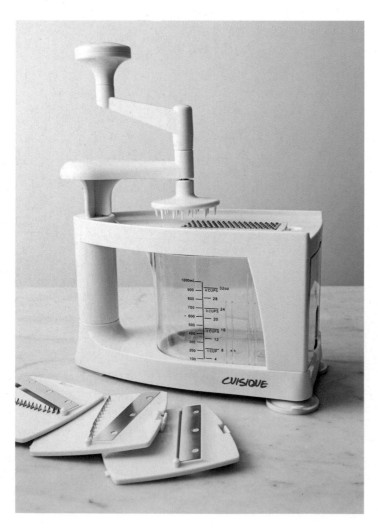

USING AN ENCLOSED SPIRALIZER

Check your instruction manual as the assembly and usage instructions vary greatly depending on the model you use. Below is a typical portable lidded version.

1 Lift up the lid; this may be hinged and permanently attached, or may be removable for easy washing. If not already in place, slot in the attachment spike, making sure that it will rotate when you turn the handle.

2 Unless you want to spiralize directly on to a serving plate or into a bowl or pan, attach the container bowl to the spiralizer, twisting and clicking into position. Double-check it is properly attached before you start to spiralize.

3 Open the lidded top of the spiralizer and attach the prepared vegetable or fruit (see the guide on pages 20–51) on to the centre blade at the bottom. Close the lid; the spikes in the lid will stick into the vegetable and hold it firmly in place.

4 Choose the blade by turning the knob on the side of the spiralizer; different numbers or letters on the dial indicate the different blades, so refer to your instruction manual.

5 Turn the handle clockwise to spiralize, so that the noodles fall into the bottom storage container. Discard the small left-over piece of vegetable in the top compartment (or see pages 52–53 for ways to use).

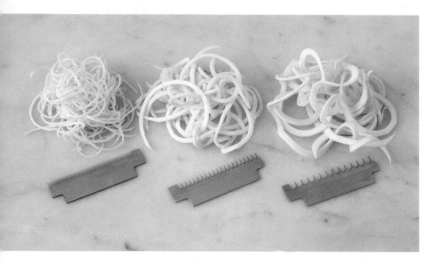

Adapting blades for noodle sizes

Blade sizes vary from model to model and recipes in this book use very fine (1mm/1⁄32in), fine (2mm/1⁄12in), medium (3mm/1⁄8in) and thick (4mm/1⁄6in) blades. Your spiralizer may have slightly different sized blades, so choose whichever is closest.

LEFT: Most vertical spiralizers have three or four interchangeable metal comb-like blades which are slotted into position, then held in place with a metal screw. The finest blade produces much thinner noodles than most horizontal spiralizers. These should last for several years, but it is usually easy to buy replacement blades when needed.

ABOVE: Hand-held spiralizers can be used to make thin and medium-thickness vegetable noodles. The blade with the most triangular cutters makes spaghetti-sized noodles, about 2–3mm/1⁄12–1⁄8in thick and the other larger noodles, about 4–5mm/1⁄6–1⁄4in.

ABOVE: Enclosed spiralizers usually have four blades. These produce fine angel-hair or vermicelli-type noodles, spaghetti-sized noodles, thin ribbons and thick ribbons.

STORAGE

Most vegetable noodles can be made in advance and stored. Keep them in a lidded glass or plastic bowl or a sealed plastic bag in the vegetable drawer of the refrigerator (the length of storage time varies depending on the vegetable). Avoid using plastic when storing brightly coloured vegetables as they may stain the container. Fruit and vegetables such as celeriac, plantain, apples and pears oxidize (turn brown) once cut, so should be used immediately after preparation.

Creating noodles without a spiralizer

While a spiralizer is a versatile gadget which can quickly produce all sorts of thin, thick and ribbon-type noodles, there are other kitchen tools which can be used to make vegetable noodles.

JULIENNE PEELERS
This compact, inexpensive hand-held tool is usually made from stainless steel and looks like an ordinary vegetable peeler, but it has a tooth-like rather than a flat blade. When pulled from top to bottom of a vegetable it will cut even-sized straight noodles, the width of a matchstick. It works particularly well on courgettes (zucchini), carrots and cucumbers. You can create wide vegetable ribbons using an ordinary vegetable peeler in the same way.

MANDOLINES
These kitchen tools have been around for many years and were probably the precursor of the spiralizer. They have blades set in a plastic, wooden or stainless steel surround and are used for cutting very fine slices. Often the width of the slices is determined by the angle at which the plastic, wooden or stainless steel beds facing the blade are set and can be adjusted with wing-nuts on either side of the frame.

Some have blades for cutting julienne strips, with others you can create julienne strips by slicing a vegetable one way, gathering up the pieces and slicing them again with the original cuts running at right angles to the blade.

More modern versions usually have a finger guard although original ones do not, so great care must be taken when slicing; hold the vegetable firmly and pass it across the blade, using the heel of your hand to push.

TOP: Julienne peeler (left), Vegetable peeler (right). ABOVE: Mandoline.

CLEANING YOUR SPIRALIZER
It's important to clean your spiralizer immediately after use, especially after preparing brightly coloured vegetables such as beetroot (beets) or carrots, or you may find it stains or yellows. Some are sold with their own cleaning brush; otherwise a small soft-bristled brush or toothbrush (you can buy 'economy' or 'value' ones relatively cheaply) will clean the hard-to-reach parts such as the teeth on the handle and metal blades when you need to. Take care when cleaning the blades as these are very sharp. Often, you will only need to quickly wash in hot soapy water, rinse under running water and leave to air-dry, then re-assemble ready for future use. If your spiralizer does stain, it can be cleaned by adding a few drops of mild bleach to the washing-up water and thoroughly rinsing afterwards. Many spiralizers can be cleaned in the dishwasher, but do check your instruction manual before doing this.

SPIRALIZER SAFETY
As with any cutting tool, spiralizer blades are extremely sharp, so treat them as carefully as you would when using and washing a knife. Small hand-held spiralizers have a safety cap that allows you to feed the last little piece of vegetable through the blade; don't forget to use it! Most horizontal spiralizers have blades fixed in a plastic casing, so you never have to touch them. Take care when slotting them in position and avoid removing the last bits of spiralized vegetables with your fingers. When washing blades it's a good idea to wear rubber gloves which will protect you from cutting yourself.

Courgettes (zucchini)

Courgettes are probably the easiest vegetable to spiralize. The long strands make a deliciously low-calorie alternative to pasta noodles and this is high on the list of reasons why so many choose to buy a spiralizer. Simply baby marrows (large zucchini), courgettes are part of the 'summer squash' family and have the best flavour when they are small and young and before the seeds inside start to develop. As well as the more familiar dark glossy green variety, courgettes come in an array of colours from pale stripy green to a deep golden yellow. Available in supermarkets all year round, their natural growing season is from summer to autumn, so this is the time when they will be less expensive and at their best. If you have a sunny patch in your garden, courgettes are worth cultivating and will provide a considerable yield from a modest area.

BUYING AND STORING

When selecting courgettes for spiralizing, pick the straightest ones you can find. A length of 18cm/7in by 2.5cm/1in diameter is ideal, although you can of course cut longer ones into shorter lengths to fit in the spiralizer. When buying, courgettes should feel firm and not very flexible, with smooth and shiny skins. Buy in small quantities, store in the vegetable drawer of the refrigerator and use within 3–4 days.

How to spiralize

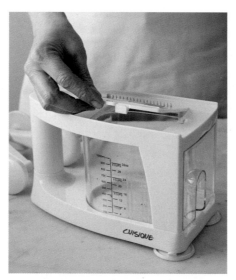

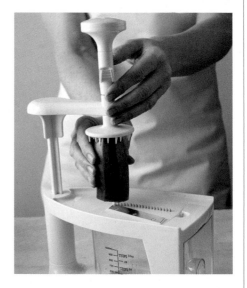

1 To prepare courgettes, rinse under cold water and pat dry, then simply slice off both ends with a sharp knife, cutting as straight and evenly as possible. There's no need to peel them; the skins are tender and will add colour to your dish.

2 If the courgette is too long to fit on the spiralizer, or if it is crooked, rather than straight, cut it in half to make two shorter straighter pieces. This will help ensure you create long strands rather than short shredded pieces. Slot your chosen blade into position on the spiralizer.

3 Securely centre the courgette on the spiralizer and turn the handle continuously in a clockwise direction to create courgette noodles or ribbons. These can be cut into shorter, more manageable lengths if you like, using clean kitchen scissors. Discard the left-over piece of courgette after spiralizing.

RIGHT and BELOW: Courgettes are easy to spiralize into long noodles and take only a minute or two to cook in boiling water.

HOW TO SERVE

Raw: Served raw, spiralized courgettes are both tender and crisp at the same time. Thin and medium noodles and slices can all be served raw and are good tossed in vinaigrette or a lemony dressing. For every spiralized courgette, whisk together 15ml/1 tbsp extra virgin oil, 5ml/1 tsp balsamic vinegar or lemon juice, salt and ground black pepper. Drizzle over the courgettes, mix well and serve within 15 minutes of making or the courgettes will start to soften. If you want to prepare in advance, you can spiralize the courgettes and make the dressing up to 24 hours ahead (store the courgettes in a sealed plastic container or bag in the salad drawer of the refrigerator), then mix together a few minutes before serving.

Boil: Drop the spiralized courgette noodles in a pan of boiling lightly salted water or stock and cook for 2 minutes for medium noodles or slices and 1–2 minutes for thin noodles.

Steam: Place the spiralized courgettes in a steamer over boiling water and cook for 3–4 minutes for medium noodles or slices and 2–3 minutes for thin noodles. The timings will depend on the amount you are steaming and how tender you like your vegetables, so check after the shortest time and cook a little longer if necessary. Courgettes have a high water content, so some liquid will leach out after steaming. Allow for this when serving as an alternative to pasta noodles, and make the sauce just a little thicker.

Stir-fry: This is a great way to cook spiralized courgettes, as some of the water content will evaporate as you cook. Use a good quality large non-stick frying pan, skillet or wok. Add 5–10ml/2–3 tsp virgin olive or sunflower oil and heat for a few minutes. Add the courgettes and cook over a medium-high heat for 2–3 minutes for thin noodles and 3 minutes for slices or medium noodles, stirring frequently. Add seasoning and a pinch of dried chilli flakes if liked at the beginning of cooking or a crushed clove of garlic halfway through cooking. A squeeze of lemon or lime juice after cooking works well if you are serving with fish, grilled or broiled chicken.

You can also steam-fry courgettes in less oil or no oil at all in a non-stick pan. Heat the pan with a few drops of oil, if liked over a medium heat. Add the courgettes, stir for a few seconds and then cover with a lid. Cook for 1 minute, then quickly stir and replace the lid. Continue cooking for a further minute. Remove the lid, then stir and season. Turn up the heat a little and cook for a few more seconds, stirring frequently, to allow some or all of the juices to evaporate.

Keep-it: Spiralized courgettes will keep for 3–4 days in a sealed plastic bag or airtight container in the refrigerator.

NUTRITIONAL NOTES

Courgettes have a water content of around 95%, so make an excellent low-carbohydrate and low-calorie alternative to pasta noodles. At just 17 calories per 100g/3½oz (an average 18cm/7in courgette weighs about 200g/7oz and will serve one), courgettes contain no saturated fats or cholesterol. They are rich in vitamins A and C and antioxidants, especially the golden-skin varieties. In addition, they are a source of potassium which helps to counteract the effects of sodium (salt) and therefore reduce high blood pressure and the risk of stroke.

Potatoes

A spiralizer is a fantastic way to produce low-carbohydrate alternatives to starchy foods such as pasta and potatoes, but there's no need to forgo the humble potato altogether; it includes both protein and fibre, vitamins B and C, iron and potassium. Using a spiralizer enables you to cook potatoes in creative ways for both everyday meals and occasional treats.

BUYING AND STORING

There are thousands of different varieties of potatoes and these are less seasonal than they used to be, with 'new' potatoes and 'earlies' being produced not just in the spring, but in greenhouse conditions in the middle of winter. Differences between potatoes are not so obvious in terms of flavour, as in texture. Some are 'floury', others 'waxy' which mean they will retain their shape after cooking, so it's important to choose the right variety according to the dish you are making. Generally, even-shaped medium or large potatoes are best for spiralizing as there will be less wastage, but you can cut scrubbed new potatoes in fine thin slices as long as they are at least 6cm/2½in long.

For spiralizing, it is best to select your own potatoes, rather than buying in a pre-packed bag. Even-shaped ones will spiralize better and should be firm without any bruised, soft or green patches. Stored in a cool, dry dark place, they should keep for a couple of weeks.

How to spiralize

1 Potatoes can be peeled or left unpeeled when spiralizing (if unpeeled, make sure you scrub them thoroughly and cut out any blemishes). Slice off both ends with a sharp knife, cutting as straight and evenly as possible.

2 If necessary, cut the potato across the middle into two shorter pieces, depending on the size that will fit in your spiralizer. If you want to make single potato slices, rather than joined concertina slices, make a lengthways cut through to the middle of the potato.

3 Slot your chosen blade into position and securely centre the potato on the spiralizer. Turn the handle continuously in a clockwise direction to create single or concertina-like slices or noodles.

RIGHT: A spiralizer will slice potatoes into different thicknesses.

HOW TO SERVE
Although you can't steam or boil potato noodles as they would stick together and have a gluey texture, you can gently fry them. Melt 15g/½oz butter plus 15ml/1 tbsp sunflower or olive oil in a large non-stick frying pan or wok. Add up to 250g/10oz potato noodles cut with a 3mm/⅛in (medium) blade and gently cook for 6–10 minutes, stirring frequently until tender and lightly browned in places. Sprinkle with a little salt if liked and serve straight away. Noodles and slices can also be incorporated into many recipes, or made into potato cakes (page 148), delicious curly fries (page 184), potato kugel (page 185) and latkes (186). Thin single slices can be made into potato galettes (page 132).

Note: To prevent potatoes and other root vegetables discoloring after peeling, immerse them in a bowl of cold water with a dash of lemon juice.

NUTRITIONAL NOTES
Potatoes are high in complex carbohydrates, so provide sustained energy. They also include protein and fibre and vitamins B and C, plus small amounts of iron and potassium.

Sweet potatoes

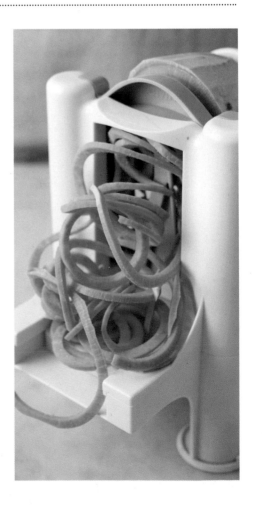

A root vegetable that resembles a potato, although the two are not related, sweet potatoes are native to the tropical Americas and sometimes referred to as 'yams' in the USA. As their name suggests, they have a slightly sweet flavour and creamy texture that works well in savoury dishes. Although sweet potatoes can be baked in their skins, they should be thinly peeled before spiralizing.

BUYING AND STORING
Try to choose even-shaped medium to large sweet potatoes with unblemished skins and store in a cool dark place, where they will keep for a week or so.

HOW TO SERVE
Sweet potatoes can be prepared and cooked in exactly the same way as normal potatoes, but cook more quickly. Their sweet flavour works well in many Caribbean dishes and curries.

NUTRITIONAL NOTES
Like ordinary potatoes, these are a good source of starchy carbohydrate and also contain vitamin C and potassium. There are two types; one has cream flesh and the other orange. The orange-flesh variety has a higher nutritional content as it is an excellent source of the antioxidant beta-carotene.

Broccoli stems

These are often discarded when cooking broccoli florets, but can easily be spiralized into noodles and added to other vegetable noodles such as courgette (zucchini) or carrot noodles to stretch them further. They have a delicious flavour, not unlike asparagus. Trim the ends of the broccoli stem as straight as possible and thinly peel (or a little thicker if the stem is tough) a layer from the outside of the stem and discard. Either slice with the spiralizer slicing blade or spiralize into noodles with the fine (2mm/1/12in) or medium (3mm/1/8in) blade. You should end up with a small handful of noodles which can be boiled, steamed or stir-fried; they take about the same amount of time to cook as carrot noodles and just a little longer than courgette noodles.

NUTRITIONAL NOTES
Broccoli is a member of the cruciferous vegetable family and is packed with phytochemicals which numerous studies have shown are anticarcinogenic. Broccoli contains almost as much calcium as milk. It also contains B vitamins, vitamin C and folate, in addition to zinc, iron and potassium.

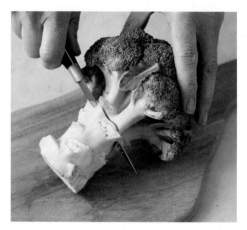

ABOVE: Choose broccoli with thick stems and cut close to the florets.

ABOVE: Cut off any knobbly bits and peel to get a smooth straight stem.

Celeriac

This large knobbly-shaped root vegetable is a member of the celery family, hence its name. The flesh is a creamy white colour. Choose a firm small to medium-sized celeriac, avoiding any that are discolored, and store in the salad drawer of the refrigerator where it will keep for a week or two.

To spiralize, use a sharp knife to top and tail, then generously peel off the thick skin. Once cut, quickly drop the noodles or slices into a bowl of cold water with a squeeze of lemon or lime juice or a spoonful of white wine vinegar. Finely spiralized noodles are delicious raw in salads or can be cooked in lightly salted boiling water for 3–4 minutes, until tender. Drain well and toss in a little butter.

NUTRITIONAL NOTES
Like celery, celeriac is a diuretic, a good source of fibre and low in calories, containing just 42 calories in 100g/3½oz. It contains vitamin C, vitamin K, calcium and iron.

Fennel

With a sweet aniseed flavour and crisp texture, fennel can be used raw in salads, added to stir-fries or gently braised until tender and served as an accompaniment to fish and chicken. It can be thinly sliced with a spiralizer in exactly the same way as cabbage. Resembling squat celery, fennel has thick ridged stalks. Eat as fresh as possible after purchase, although it will keep in the salad drawer for several days. Immediately after spiralizing, toss in vinaigrette or add to a bowl of water with a dash of lemon juice or vinegar to stop the cut surfaces turning brown. Fennel contains more phytoestrogen than most vegetables which helps protect against breast and prostate cancers. It is also thought to aid digestion.

NUTRITIONAL NOTES
Fennel has diuretic properties and can aid digestion. It is also low in calories, with an average bulb containing around 70 calories. In addition it contains good amounts of beta-carotene and folate as well as vitamin C. It contains a unique combination of phytonutrients that give it strong antioxidant activity.

ABOVE: Spiralize fennel without the top stem and feathery fronds, cut-side down.

ABOVE: To avoid the fennel turning brown, pour over lemon juice immediately.

Parsnips

A similar shape but slightly larger than carrots, creamy-coloured parsnips can be spiralized in exactly the same way. Slightly sweet, nutty and full-flavoured, buy medium-sized parsnips; small ones are difficult to spiralize and very large ones may have a woody texture and a strong flavour. Avoid any which are soft or have brown patches and store in a cool airy dark place for up to a week.

To spiralize, top and tail, then either scrub the skin with a soft brush under cold running water or thinly peel. Either stir-fry in a little oil for 3–4 minutes until tender or toss spiralized noodles in oil, season well and roast in a non-stick roasting pan at 350°F/180°C/Gas 4 for about 10 minutes until tender, turning halfway through so that it cooks evenly.

NUTRITIONAL NOTES
Parsnips contain both vitamins C and E which are a powerful antioxidant combination, as well as folic acid, iron and potassium.

Butternut squash

This large pear-shaped winter squash has a golden skin and deep golden flesh, with a sweet creamy nutty flavour. Similiar to pumpkin, it has a lot of seeds but these are concentrated in the more bulbous end of the squash, so the top two-thirds can easily be spiralized. The inedible skin is tough and should be thinly peeled.

BUYING AND STORING
A ripe butternut squash will weigh about 1kg/2lb and should be a light orange colour without any tinges of green. The skin may have rough patches, but these will be where the squash has rested on the soil and are not a problem. Check for any cuts or bruises, as once damaged the squash will deteriorate quickly. Keep in a cool, dark, dry place or in the salad drawer of the refrigerator for up to a week. For spiralizing, choose a butternut squash which has a smaller proportion of bulbous end to the stem end and with a fat stem end, as this section is much easier to spiralize into long strands of noodles. As with all vegetables for spiralizing, straight and even-shaped produce is best.

How to spiralize

1 Slice off both ends with a sharp knife, cutting as straight and evenly as possible; take care as butternut squash is hard and tough, so make a shallow cut first before slicing to prevent the knife slipping. Stand the butternut squash upright on the wider end and thinly peel away the skin with a vegetable peeler.

2 Cut off the bulbous end containing all the seeds; this is usually about the bottom third. Cut this piece of butternut squash into quarters, lengthways, and use a teaspoon or knife to scoop out the seeds and fibres surrounding them. If the rest of the butternut squash is too large (this may be the case if you are using a vertical spiralizer), cut it in half widthways to make two shorter pieces.

3 Slot your chosen blade into position, then securely centre the first piece of butternut squash on the spiralizer. Turn the handle continuously in a clockwise direction to create butternut squash noodles. Spiralize each piece in the same way, one at a time. It may not be possible to make long noodles, but you should be able to get shorter crescent-shaped slices.

HOW TO SERVE

Roast: Toss spiralized noodles in a little sunflower oil and season well with salt and pepper. Roast in a non-stick roasting pan at 400°F/200°C/Gas 6 for 8–10 minutes until tender, turning halfway through, so that it cooks evenly.

Sauté: Heat a little butter, coconut or sunflower oil in a large non-stick frying pan, skillet or wok and add the spiralized noodles. Cook over a medium heat, stirring frequently for 3–4 minutes, then add a spoonful or two of stock or water and cook for a further 2–3 minutes or until tender.

Boil: Drop the spiralized noodles in lightly salted boiling water or stock and simmer for 4–5 minutes, until tender.

Steam: Place the spiralized noodles in a steamer over boiling water and cook for 6–7 minutes for medium (3mm/⅛in noodles) and 5–6 minutes for thin (2mm/¹⁄₁₂in) noodles.

Keep-it: Spiralized butternut squash can be kept for up to 5 days in an airtight container or a sealed plastic bag in the salad drawer of the refrigerator, but may lose its crisp texture, so is best freshly prepared.

NUTRITIONAL NOTES

Butternut squash, like most orange coloured vegetables, is rich in antioxidants. It contains high levels of vitamins A and C and small amounts of numerous minerals including iron, zinc, calcium, potassium and phosphorous. At 45 calories per 100g/3½oz, it makes a good alternative to starchy carbohydrates such as potatoes or pasta.

SPIRALIZED RICE

This vegetable 'rice' is made from vegetable noodles and can be used instead of ordinary rice or grains in many dishes. Most vegetables can be used to make rice, however when turning vegetables with a high water content such as squash and courgettes (zucchini) into rice, take care not to over-process; harder vegetables such as carrots and turnips can be made slightly smaller.

To make vegetable 'rice' place spiralized vegetable noodles in a food processor and pulse for 10–15 seconds or until rice-like. The rice can be used raw, or sautéed in a little butter or oil until tender. It can also be added to dishes such as soups and casseroles, but avoid steaming or the rice will become mushy.

LEFT: Butternut squash has a hard texture so apply a little more pressure when turning the handle to spiralize into long thin or thick noodles or ribbons.

Beetroot (beets)

Beetroot spiralizes beautifully into long curly deep ruby-red strands. It has a slightly earthy flavour and a dramatic colour which works well in many dishes, although its tendency to 'bleed' can mar the appearance of others and makes careful preparation a necessity if you want to avoid red-stained hands, work surfaces and clothing. Beetroot has a natural sweetness which makes it a perfect partner for ingredients such as salty cheeses or for combining with apples and other sweet fruit and vegetables, or slightly bitter ones such as chicory (Belgian endive). It is often served with slightly aniseedy herbs such as dill, chervil and tarragon and nuts, especially walnuts and hazelnuts. It features in both Russian and Scandinavian cuisine, notably in stews and soups such as borsch. Often pickled in vinegar, fresh beetroot is good raw, roasted and sautéed. Less commonly available are golden and white varieties although the taste differs little between them. Chioggia beetroot, also known as 'candy cane' beet as it has alternating spirals of red and cream, looks stunning when spiralized. The mangle, also known as mangel-wurzel, is a chance hybrid of beetroot and chard and is a large swollen reddish-yellow root. Small ones can be served in the same way as beetroot.

How to spiralize

1 If you want to protect your hands from the staining red juices, wear rubber or plastic gloves, or wash your hands immediately after preparation. Using a sharp knife, slice off the stalk and root ends as evenly and as straight as possible.

2 Thinly peel the beetroot; it should only be necessary to thickly peel if it is old and slightly fibrous. Very young firm beetroot may not need peeling and can simply be scrubbed with a soft brush to remove any dirt.

3 Slot your chosen blade into position; beetroot can be cut into any sized noodle or concertina slices if preferred. Securely centre the beetroot on the spiralizer. If there is a thinner end, place this at the front, so the spikes can grip the wider end more firmly. Turn the handle continuously in a clockwise direction to create beetroot noodles or slices.

BUYING AND STORING

Choose round evenly shaped beetroot for spiralizing; small beetroot are sweeter and more tender than large ones, but there will be more wastage, so it is better to opt for medium-sized ones. Make sure that they are firm and not shrivelled and store in a cool, dark place; the salad drawer of the refrigerator is fine. Providing they are fresh when purchased, they should keep for a week or two. If you grow beetroot or buy with the green tops still attached, these make a tasty green vegetable and can be steamed or stir-fried until tender.

HOW TO SERVE

Raw: Very thin (1mm/¹⁄₃₂in) or thin (2mm/¹⁄₁₂in) beetroot noodles are delicious in salads and coleslaws, but be aware that the juices will leach and make the surrounding ingredients a pink colour (in fact this can look attractive). Toss the noodles in a honey and orange dressing or a yogurt and mayonnaise mixture.

Boil: Beetroot noodles can be boiled but some of the red colour will be lost in the cooking liquid, so this method is best used where both the beetroot and cooking liquid will be used; the cooking liquid is excellent added to dark-coloured soups and casseroles where it will add both a rich colour and slightly earthy flavour. Drop the noodles into boiling lightly salted water or vegetable stock and simmer for 2–3 minutes or until tender. Drain well.

Sauté: Heat a little coconut or sunflower oil in a large non-stick frying pan, skillet or wok. Add the spiralized beetroot and season with salt and ground black pepper. Cook for about 5 minutes, stirring frequently. For a slightly sweet and caramelized flavour, add 5ml/1 tsp honey, maple syrup or agave sryup for the last 2 minutes of cooking time.

Roast: Place the spiralized beetroot in a roasting pan and drizzle with a little olive oil or melted coconut oil. Season and toss the beetroot with your hands to coat evenly. Cook at 200°C/400°F/Gas 6 for 10–12 minutes or until cooked.

Keep-it: Spiralized beetroot can be kept for up to 2 days in an airtight container in the refrigerator. Place it in a plastic bag first, so that it doesn't stain the container. If you are using the spiralized noodles raw in a salad, toss them in a squeeze of fresh orange juice to keep the noodles moist and flexible.

NUTRITIONAL NOTES

With 45 calories per 100g/3½oz, beetroot have recently been praised for their cholesterol-lowering properties, although you do have to consume fairly large amounts daily for this to be effective. They contain unique antioxidants which offer protection against coronary heart disease and stroke. Beetroot contains iron, calcium and vitamins A and C; these are all at their highest levels when it is eaten raw.

ABOVE and FAR LEFT: Beetroot noodles are delicious served raw or lightly roasted until tender.

Carrots

The earliest carrots were deep red or purple in colour and served as a dessert, sweetened with honey. They are still used in cakes, desserts such as Indian carrot halva and made into jams. While it is still possible to buy red and purple carrots and yellow, green and white ones as well, these are usually now regarded as novelty vegetables and priced accordingly, and it is the familiar orange-coloured carrot that is found on supermarket and greengrocers' shelves. Originally bred by patriotic Dutch growers in the 17th century, because orange was the national colour of their independent state, they found that unlike early carrots these tended to have just one long straight root so were easier to prepare and cook, and their popularity grew.

BUYING AND STORING

For spiralizing it is preferable to buy the straightest largest carrots you can; shorter fatter ones are better than long thin ones. When buying, they should feel firm and have no traces of dampness which may indicate decay. Carrots which still have their green feathery tops should look fresh and not wilted. If you buy supermarket carrots in a plastic bag, either open up the bag or remove the carrots completely so that air can circulate and store them in the salad drawer of the refrigerator. Use within a week of purchase. Do try some of the different coloured carrots if you come across them; they look stunning made into noodles and served raw (but lose much of their colour when cooked), especially purple ones which often have a yellow core and make lovely stripy multi-coloured noodles.

HOW TO SERVE

Raw: Very thin (1mm/¹⁄₃₂in) and thin (2mm/¹⁄₁₂in) noodles are good raw in salads and work well with flavoured vinaigrettes such as orange, honey or fresh ginger. For every spiralized carrot, whisk together 15ml/1 tbsp sunflower oil, 2.5ml/½ tsp clear honey and 5ml/1 tsp white wine vinegar. Whisk in a little zested orange rind or the squeezed juice from grated fresh ginger.

Steam: Place the carrots in a steamer over boiling water and cook for 4–5 minutes for medium (3mm/¹⁄₈in) noodles and 3–4 minutes for thin (2mm/¹⁄₁₂in) noodles.

Boil: Drop medium (3mm/¹⁄₈in) or thick (4mm/¹⁄₆in) noodles or slices into boiling lightly salted water and cook for 3–4 minutes or until tender. Drain well and toss in a little melted butter if liked and season with salt and ground black pepper.

Stir-fry: Use a good quality large non-stick frying pan, skillet or wok. Add 5–10ml/2–3 tbsp coconut, sunflower or light olive oil and heat for a few minutes. Add the carrots and cook over a medium high-heat for 2–3 minutes, then add 15ml/1 tbsp vegetable stock, orange juice, or water and cook for a further minute or two until the stock has evaporated and the carrots are tender. Season well.

OPPOSITE: Carrots are one of the easiest vegetables to spiralize and are good raw and cooked. If you come across heirloom varieties in other colours do try them, as they make pretty and interesting noodles.

NUTRITIONAL NOTES

The large amount of beta-carotene in carrots make this vegetable an excellent source of vitamin A; more beta-carotene is absorbed by the body if the carrots are cooked rather than served raw. Carrots also have cardiovascular benefits, as do many yellow and orange vegetables, with no fat or cholesterol, and they have just 12 calories per 100g/3½oz.

How to spiralize

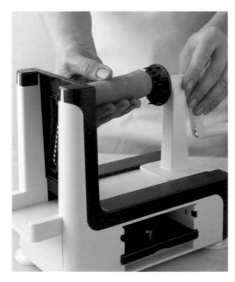

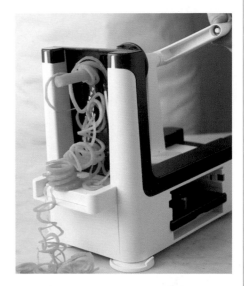

1 Peel the carrots as thinly as possible, or just scrub them well if the carrots are young, then slice off both ends with a sharp knife, cutting as straight and evenly as possible.

2 If the carrot is too long to fit on the spiralizer, or if it is slightly crooked rather than straight, cut it in half to make two shorter straighter pieces. This will help to ensure that you create long strands rather than short shredded pieces. Slot your chosen blade into position, then securely centre the carrot on the spiralizer.

3 Turn the handle continuously in a clockwise direction to create carrot noodles or ribbons. These can be cut into shorter, more manageable lengths if you like, using clean kitchen scissors. Discard the left-over piece of carrot after spiralizing.

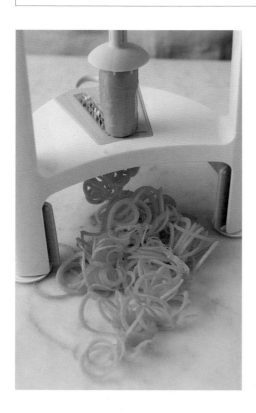

Mooli (daikon)

Mooli is similar in size, shape and appearance to a large white parsnip. It is often carved into beautiful edible sculptures and used as a garnish in oriental restaurants. This large white radish has a mild peppery flavour which works well raw in salads and can also be cooked and used as a vegetable or in soups; it is unique in that it soaks up the flavour of the stock or sauce it is cooked with. It is often made into a bright yellow Japanese pickle known as Takuan. Red-skinned mooli are also available and add an attractive colour to many dishes.

BUYING AND STORING

Available all year round, the natural growing season is during the winter and spring months. Mooli can be found in some supermarkets, as well as oriental stores and online from Japanese food suppliers. For spiralizing, choose a straight mooli, preferably a short stubby one rather than a thin elongated one, as you will get better spiral lengths. The vegetable should be firm and look fresh without any cracks or splits. Avoid any which look slightly yellow as this is an indication that the vegetable is old. If they still have the leafy tops, these should be bright green and not yellowing or dry. After purchase, trim off any leafy tops (leave a 1cm/½in stem) and store in the vegetable drawer of the refrigerator. Use within a week of purchase.

How to spiralize

1 To prepare mooli, slice off both ends with a sharp knife, cutting as straight and evenly as possible. Peel thinly, removing as little of the skin as possible. If the mooli is too long to fit on the spiralizer, or if it is crooked, cut into two lengths (or three if the mooli is very long).

2 Slot your chosen blade into position, then securely centre the first piece of mooli on the spiralizer.

3 Turn the handle continuously in a clockwise direction to create mooli noodles or ribbons. These can be cut into shorter, more manageable lengths. Discard the left-over piece of mooli after spiralizing, or you could use it to create your own tiny vegetable sculpture!

HOW TO SERVE

Raw: Serve very fine 1mm/1/32in (vermicelli/angel-hair pasta size) or thin 2mm/1/12in (spaghetti-size) noodles raw in salads or coleslaw. It works well with sweeter spiralized vegetables such as carrots and matchstick-sliced beansprouts and is good tossed in a ginger dressing. For every spiralized mooli, whisk together the squeezed juices from a 2cm/3/4in piece of peeled and grated fresh ginger, 30ml/2 tbsp mirin, 30ml/ 2 tbsp sesame oil and 15ml/1 tbsp soy sauce. Drizzle over the mooli and mix well. Chill until ready to serve.

Boil: Bring a pan of lightly salted water or stock to the boil, add thin or medium mooli noodles and cook for 2–3 minutes or until just tender but still firm. Drain well and serve instead of egg noodles.

Steam: Place the spiralized mooli in a steamer over boiling water and cook for 4 minutes for medium noodles or slices and 3–4 minutes for thin noodles. Serve tossed in a little sesame oil.

Stir-fry: This is a more traditional way to cook mooli. Use a good quality large non-stick frying pan, skillet or wok. Add 5–10ml/2–3 tsp sunflower or sesame oil and heat for a few minutes. Add the mooli and cook over a medium-high heat for 2–3 minutes for thin noodles and 3–4 minutes for slices or medium noodles, stirring frequently. Add seasoning and finely chopped fresh root ginger, if liked.

ABOVE and ABOVE LEFT: Mooli is equally good served lightly boiled or raw in a salad. Red-skinned mooli adds a pink tinge to the dish!

NUTRITIONAL NOTES

One of the very low-calorie root vegetables, mooli contains just 16 calories per 100g/3½oz. It is a good source of several vitamins, notably vitamin C, and minerals. Like many other cruciferous and brassica family vegetables, it contains an antioxidant compound called sulforaphane, which may inhibit cancer-cell growth. Mooli is believed to have active enzymes which help with digestion.

Kohlrabi

This green-tinged or purple flattened globe-shaped vegetable looks like a root, but is actually a swollen stem which grows above the ground, with green leaves on top of sprouting stalks. Kohlrabi is sometimes known as a turnip-cabbage; the name is an indication of its crisp texture and nutty, mildly cabbage-like flavour. The green-tinged varieties tend to be more well-flavoured and tender and the purple ones slightly more spicy, with a similar flavour to mild radish. Both are excellent for spiralizing and make long attractive white strands.

Kohlrabi is popular in Eastern European cuisine as it tolerates frost and can be stored for a long time, but also grows in hot regions. It can grow quite large but is usually harvested when small as the texture becomes tougher as it matures.

BUYING AND STORING

Choose kohlrabi no bigger than a small apple for the best flavour and texture, but not much smaller for spiralizing or you will get short strands rather than long spirals and there will be more wastage. Kohlrabi are often sold with just a few cut stems sticking up, but if you manage to buy with the green leaves still

NUTRITIONAL NOTES

Kohlrabi contains around 27 calories per 100g/3½oz, roughly a quarter of that in potatoes, no cholesterol and a negligible amount of fat. As well as health-promoting phytochemicals, it contains good amounts of many B-vitamins and several minerals, notably potassium, which can help counteract the effects of sodium (salt) and help reduce high blood pressure.

How to spiralize

1 To prepare kohlrabi, thinly slice off the top and the root end with a sharp knife, cutting as straight and evenly as possible.

2 Peel thinly if the kohlrabi are fairly small and young (you may be able to leave the skins on if they are very young and fresh), and more thickly if they are larger and older as these will have tougher, more fibrous skins.

3 Slot your chosen blade into position, then securely centre the kohlrabi on the spiralizer and turn the handle continuously in a clockwise direction to create kohlrabi noodles or ribbons. These can be cut into shorter, more manageable lengths if you like, using clean kitchen scissors. Discard the left-over piece of kohlrabi after spiralizing or use in another recipe.

attached, these can be steamed whole or shredded and stir-fried. Keep kohlrabi in a cool place such as the salad drawer of the refrigerator; they will keep for several weeks, although are best eaten within a week of purchase.

HOW TO SERVE

Raw: Thin (2mm/1/12in) kohlrabi noodles can be used in salads or in coleslaw instead of traditional white cabbage and have a crisp texture and mild peppery flavour. Spiralized kohlrabi is good served with spiralized apples and carrots with a very light coating of creamy dressing; blend 15ml/1 tbsp mayonnaise with 30ml/2 tbsp natural (plain) yogurt, 5ml/1 tsp creamed horseradish sauce and seasoning to taste for every 225g/8oz spiralized vegetables and apple.

Boil: Drop spiralized kohlrabi into boiling lightly salted water and cook for 2–3 minutes for thin (spaghetti-sized) noodles or slices and 3–4 minutes for medium and thick noodles. Drain well. If serving in a soup or sauce allow for a little juice to leach out after cooking, making the consistency of the finished dish a little thinner.

Steam: Place the spiralized kohlrabi in a steamer over boiling water and cook for 4–6 minutes until tender. The timing will depend on the amount you are steaming and how tender you like your vegetables, so check after the shortest time and cook a little longer if necessary.

Stir-fry: Cook in a large non-stick frying pan, skillet or wok in a little melted butter, coconut oil or sunflower oil (don't use a strongly flavoured oil such as virgin olive oil as it will overpower the subtle flavour) over a medium high heat for 2–3 minutes. Caraway seeds work well with kohlrabi, so sprinkle over 5ml/ 1 tsp for 4 servings, towards the end of cooking time. If liked, add a little double (heavy) cream or soya cream and bubble for a few minutes to reduce. Season with salt and ground black pepper before serving.

Roast: This brings out the sweetness of the vegetable and makes a lower-calorie version of potato fries. For 4 servings, spiralize 2 large (apple-sized) kohlrabi into medium-sized noodles. Put in a bowl and drizzle with 30ml/2 tbsp sunflower oil, 10ml/2 tbsp ground paprika, salt and ground black pepper. Mix well then place in a heated roasting pan and cook at 200°C/400°F/ Gas 6 for 10 minutes. Turn, then bake for a further 10-15 minutes, turning every 5 minutes until brown and crisp.

Keep-it: Spiralized kohlrabi will keep in a plastic bag or airtight container in the refrigerator (spray with a little cold water to keep moist) for up to 5 days after spiralizing.

KOHLRABI DAUPHINOISE

This makes a lower-carbohydrate alternative to potatoes. Spiralize 900g/2lb peeled kohlrabi with the slicing blade and cut the thin concertina slices into short lengths with kitchen scissors. Arrange in a greased baking dish about 20 x 25cm/8 x 10in, overlapping the slices. Pour over 250ml/8fl oz/1 cup well-flavoured vegetable or chicken stock. Cover the top with a piece of baking parchment and bake at 160°C/325°F/Gas 3 for 1½ hours. Remove the baking parchment and bake for a further 20–30 minutes or until the kohlrabi is tender and the top golden brown.

BELOW: A light sprinkling of caraway seeds brings out the flavour of stir-fried ribbons of kohlrabi.

Peppers

These brightly coloured vegetables, also known as bell peppers or capsicums, are all essentially the same variety but at different stages of ripeness; green being the youngest which if left on the plant would eventually turn through orange to red with a much sweeter flavour. Other strains have been developed and you can also find white, black and purple peppers, although the latter two turn green when cooked, so are best used raw. White peppers turn ivory as they ripen and become sweeter, whereas purple ones have a similar flavour to green peppers, and turn a reddish-black colour. Peppers feature in many traditional dishes and cuisines and are a main ingredient of Mediterranean dishes, including ratatouille and piperade, as well as being popular in Mexican, Chinese and Middle Eastern cooking. In Eastern Europe, green peppers are often combined with cucumber, onion and green chilli and mixed with sour cream to make a refreshing salad.

BUYING AND STORING

Choose short, squat, straight and even-shaped peppers for spiralizing and make sure they are very firm and 'crisp'. You can spiralize longer pointed varieties such as Romano peppers which have an even sweeter flavour, but make sure you pick a straight rather than curved one. Peppers should be glossy with an unblemished

How to spiralize

1 Trim the stalk so it is no more than 1cm/½in long (do not remove it entirely as it will keep the top of the pepper stable and give the spiralizer spike more grip).

2 Cut a slice from the bottom of the pepper with a sharp knife, as straight as possible. Use a small knife or teaspoon to scrape out the white core and seeds.

3 Slot your chosen blade into position; you can use a noodle or a slicing blade. Securely centre the pepper on the spiralizer, firmly pushing the stalk end into the spiked holder. Turn the handle continuously in a clockwise direction to create thin slices or pepper noodles. These can be cut into shorter lengths.

ABOVE and RIGHT: Combining different peppers adds vibrant colour to all sorts of dishes, whether cooked or in a raw salad.

skin and no signs of wrinkling. They will keep in salad drawer in the refrigerator for up to a week, ideally stored in a plastic bag with the top left open to keep in the moisture, but still allowing a little air to circulate.

HOW TO SERVE
Raw: Spiralized noodles and slices are delicious in salads.

Stir-fry: Add noodles and slices to stir-fries; they take 2–3 minutes to cook over a moderate heat and should be tender, but with a slight bite. Cooking increases the sweetness and peppers work particularly well in Mediterranean dishes with tomatoes and courgettes (zucchini) and in oriental dishes with beansprouts.

Steamed: If you want to cook peppers without added fat, steam over a pan of boiling water for 4–5 minutes until tender. Try adding them to a fresh home-made tomato sauce and serving with pasta.

Roasted: Toss spiralized peppers in a little olive oil and spread over a non-stick roasting pan. Roast in the oven at 200°C/400°F/Gas 6 for 12–15 minutes, until tender and lightly charred, turning halfway through cooking.

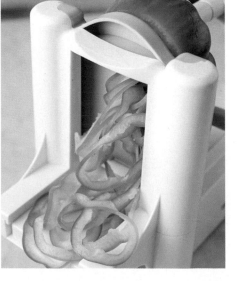

NUTRITIONAL NOTES
A single pepper has just 30–40 calories and is very high in vitamins A and C with significant amounts of vitamin B6 as well as calcium, phosphorus and iron. A great source of antioxidants, peppers contain lycopene which helps reduce the risk of certain cancers.

Cucumbers

With a high water content of around 96%, this refreshing vegetable is usually served fresh and raw, and along with lettuce and tomatoes was once considered a vital component of an 'English' salad. It features in many cuisines around the world and is popular combined with yogurt and garlic to make a cooling Indian 'raita' or Turkish 'cacik'. As well as serving raw, cucumber can be lightly cooked as a vegetable in its own right, or used as a base for a chilled summer soup.

The most common variety is the dark fairly smooth-skinned green cucumber found in supermarkets, but the skin can also be ridged or bumpy. Pale green and yellow-green varieties are also available. 'Apple cucumbers' are much shorter, almost oval in shape and are a pale green colour. They have a sweeter flavour and may be served as a fruit rather than a vegetable.

BUYING AND STORING
Pick the straightest cucumber you can find for spiralizing. It should feel firm; any that bend slightly will be less fresh as they have lost moisture. Store in the salad drawer of the refrigerator for up to 5 days. Many supermarket cucumbers are shrink-wrapped in plastic to prevent dehydration, so leave this on and if you slice off a portion, wrap the cut end in clear film or plastic wrap.

How to spiralize

1 To prepare a cucumber, wash thoroughly to remove any surface dirt and pesticide residue. Do not peel, as the skin helps with digestion and also contains most of the vitamin and mineral content. Slice off both ends with a sharp knife. Cut the cucumber into two or three shorter lengths, depending on the size that will fit in your spiralizer.

2 Slot your chosen blade into position; cucumber is better cut into medium (3mm/⅛in) or thick (4mm/⅙in) noodles or sliced. Securely centre the cucumber on the spiralizer and turn the handle continuously in a clockwise direction to create cucumber noodles or concertina-type slices. These can be cut into shorter, more manageable lengths.

3 If you want to remove moisture, place the spiralized cucumber in a colander, sieve or strainer, lightly sprinkling with salt between the layers. Leave to drain over a bowl for 15 minutes, then blot with kitchen paper.

HOW TO SERVE

Raw: Spiralized cucumber noodles and slices can be added to mixed salads, used to add moistness to sandwich fillings and make great garnishes for food such as smoked salmon and cocktail drinks. The mild flavour works particularly well with fresh herbs such as dill and mint.

Steam: Place spiralized cucumber slices in a steamer over boiling water and cook for 2 minutes or until slightly softened. Drain and season well.

Stir-fry: As cucumbers contain a lot of water, it is not possible to brown or crispen them, but this is a good way to cook spiralized cucumber slices, as some of the moisture will evaporate. Cook in a little melted butter, margarine, coconut or sesame oil over a medium heat for 2–3 minutes, stirring frequently. Both steamed and stir-fried cucumber goes well with steamed, poached, grilled, broiled or baked fish and chicken. Try cooking in a little toasted sesame oil and sprinkling with sesame seeds to serve with oriental-style dishes, or stir a spoonful of thick creamy natural (plain) yogurt into well-drained cooked cucumber to serve with spicy meals.

Keep-it: Spiralized cucumber can be kept for up to 24 hours in an airtight container or a sealed plastic bag in the salad drawer of the refrigerator, but may lose its crisp texture, so is best freshly prepared.

NUTRITIONAL NOTES
With its high water content, cucumber has just 10 calories per 100g/3½oz and contains virtually no fat, cholesterol or sodium (salt). Very mildly diuretic, it is a moderate source of vitamin C and contains small amounts of vitamins A, K and B6 as well as potassium.

ABOVE LEFT to RIGHT: Cucumbers can be spiralized into slices and medium or thick noodles. If you are serving cucumber raw, blot up some of the juices by placing between layers of kitchen paper and gently pressing. BELOW: Fresh dill is the perfect partner for raw cucumber.

Onions

Onions are the cook's greatest allies and are probably the most widely used and versatile cooking ingredient. They feature as an essential flavouring in many savoury dishes including soups, casseroles and curries. There are larger mild-tasting Spanish (Bermuda) onions with creamy-coloured flesh; smaller brown onions which are slightly stronger flavoured; white onions with papery white outer skins and flesh and a similar flavour to brown onions; and the mildest, sweetest type, red onions with their glorious reddish-purple skins and white flesh, stained red at the edges of each layer. All are perfect for spiralizing into noodles or can be cut into thin slices with the spiralizer slicing blade.

Spiralizing is an excellent way to prepare onions, as it is much quicker than slicing by hand and doesn't release the juices in the same way as chopping in a food processor (too much liquid will mean that onions steam rather than fry when cooked). The shorter time it takes to spiralize also means that you will be less exposed to the compound allyl sulfate which is produced when onions are cut and can make you cry.

BUYING AND STORING
Medium or large even-shaped onions are best for spiralizing and should be firm and fresh. Most onions have been allowed to dry out slightly after harvesting and will have crisp papery skins. Choose those which feel heavy for

How to spiralize

1 Slice off both ends with a sharp knife, cutting as straight and evenly as possible. Peel off the onion's outer papery skin.

2 Slot your chosen blade into position. Securely centre the onion on the spiralizer, firmly pushing the root end of the onion into the spiked holder. Turn the handle continuously in a clockwise direction to create onion noodles or thin slices.

3 Noodles can be cut into shorter lengths if you like, using clean kitchen scissors. Discard the left-over piece of onion after spiralizing.

their size and have dry skins (which may or not be peeling off). Avoid any which appear slightly damp, have any green powdery mould, are soft or that are beginning to sprout green shoots. Kept in a cool, dry place, onions can keep for a month or two, but you should check regularly as any decay in one will quickly spread to others.

HOW TO SERVE

Raw: Spiralized noodles and slices can be added to salads or used raw in sandwiches to add a pungent 'bite'; red onions are particularly good served in this way as they are slightly sweeter and milder than other onions and added to an acidic dressing (which will also mellow the flavour) will turn them a stunning pink colour: whisk 45ml/3 tbsp olive or sunflower oil with 15ml/1 tbsp white or red wine vinegar or lemon juice or 20ml/4 tsp balsamic vinegar in a bowl. Add the spiralized onion and toss well to coat in the dressing. Cover the bowl with clear film or plastic wrap and chill in the refrigerator for about half an hour to allow the dressing to soften the onion flavour and texture a little.

Fry: Onions can be quick-fried or slow-fried. Use the former to add a little colour and flavour when you are adding onions to a casserole or similar dish which will then be cooked for a long time. Heat oil or other fat in a frying pan or skillet over a medium heat, add the onions and cook for 3–4 minutes, stirring frequently until just starting to colour.

To slow-fry onions, cook over a very low heat for 10–15 minutes until they soften and turn a deep golden yellow colour. Stir them occasionally to prevent them sticking to the pan and browning as this will spoil the flavour. You can cover the onions with a lid or piece of baking parchment to stop steam escaping and allow them to cook even more slowly.

Roasting: Onions can be roasted in the oven with other vegetables and go particularly well with spiralized root vegetables such as sweet potatoes, butternut squash and beetroot. Place thickly spiralized onion noodles in a roasting pan, season with salt and pepper and add herbs such as rosemary or thyme. Drizzle over some olive or sunflower oil and mix together with your hands to coat. Cover with foil and cook at 180°C/350°F/Gas 4 for 30 minutes. Remove the foil, sprinkle with 2.5ml/½ tsp caster (superfine) sugar and a little balsamic vinegar, then return to the oven and cook uncovered for a further 15–25 minutes, stirring once or twice until soft and lightly browned.

BELOW: White and brown-skinned onions are good fried in a little olive oil; milder, sweeter red onions are often served raw.

Turnips and swedes (rutabaga)

These two root vegetables are members of the brassica family and can be used interchangeably in most recipes. Their flavour and texture are similar and can be sweet to slightly spicy. Turnips come in a range of colours, from pure white to yellow or purple, but usually have creamy-white skins tinged with green and white flesh, whereas swedes have yellow and purple skins and pale orange flesh. Native to northern Europe, these root vegetables have a somewhat underrated reputation as they used to be considered a food for the poor and have often suffered from over-cooking.

TURNIPS
These have a delicate nutty flavour and sweetness when young and are sometimes sold in bunches when no bigger than a golf ball in the spring and summer. For spiralizing, medium-sized turnips around the size of a small apple are preferable; avoid any which are larger than this as they lose their sweetness and develop a coarser texture as they grow. When young they have a pleasant mild peppery flavour, which develops and intensifies as they get bigger. Try to buy those with their leafy green tops intact as these are highly nutritious and good served lightly steamed or stir-fried. Turnips are usually served cooked and are delicious sautéed in a little butter or coconut oil. They are also good raw if spiralized into thin noodles or finely sliced with the slicing blade.

How to spiralize

1 To prepare both turnips and swedes, cut a thick slice off the tip and a thinner slice from the bottom to reveal the flesh. Cut as straight and evenly as possible.

2 Most swedes need to have a thick layer of skin removed, as the outer layer of flesh is usually tougher and more fibrous. Turnips can usually be peeled thinly, depending on their age and size.

3 Slot your chosen blade into position, then securely centre the vegetable on the spiralizer and turn the handle continuously in a clockwise direction to produce noodles or ribbons. Discard the left-over piece of turnip or swede or use in another recipe.

SWEDES

Swedes are grown for both their large swollen root and for their leaves. The name comes from the abbreviation of 'Swedish turnip' as they were first grown in Britain by a Scot who was sent the seeds by the king of Sweden in the late 18th century. Swedes became a popular food for both human and animal consumption. They are still enjoyed with haggis on Burn's night and in Scotland, a mashed mixture of swede and turnip (or sometimes just swede alone) is known as 'neeps' and equal quantities of potato and swede as 'clapshot'. Swede is also popular in the far south-west of Britain and is an essential ingredient of a classic Cornish pasty. The traditional way to cook swede is to boil and mash, either on their own or with potatoes or carrots, but they are equally good spiralized and served tossed in a little butter or baked, in a gratin for example. The flesh becomes sweeter with cooking and can be enhanced with warm spices such as ginger or chilli.

BUYING AND STORING

Buy hard crisp turnips and firm swedes that feel heavy for their size. If they have green tops, these should look fresh. Store in a cool, dark airy place, or in the salad drawer of the refrigerator. They should keep for at least a week.

HOW TO SERVE

Raw: Thin (2mm/¹⁄₁₂in) turnip noodles can be eaten raw in salads and coleslaw. They are good served in a dressing made with nut oil such as walnut or hazelnut.

ABOVE: Steaming is a healthy option for cooking turnips and swedes. BELOW: Balsamic vinegar and oil make an excellent marinade before roasting.

Boil: Drop spiralized turnip or swede noodles into boiling lightly salted water or vegetable stock and cook for 3–5 minutes for medium (3mm/⅛in) or thick (4mm/¹⁄₆in) noodles. Test frequently after the first 3 minutes of cooking time as they should be served when just tender and will become soggy and fall apart if over-cooked. Drain well and toss in a little butter if liked, seasoning generously.

Steam: Place the noodles in a steamer over boiling water and cook for 5–7 minutes until tender. The timing will depend on the amount you are steaming and the age of the vegetables; older ones will take a little longer to cook.

Sauté: Cook in a large non-stick frying pan or skillet in a little melted butter, coconut oil or sunflower oil (or a combination) over a medium high heat for 4–5 minutes. Add a little grated or dried ground ginger or some zested orange rind for extra flavour.

Bake: For a turnip gratin, spiralize 900g/2lb turnips using the medium (3mm/⅛in) or a thick (4mm/¹⁄₆in) noodle blade if you spiralizer has one. Cut into slightly shorter lengths and mix with 50g/2oz/½ cup grated Gruyère cheese and season with salt and pepper. Pack tightly into a greased baking dish (rub the base and sides of the dish with a cut clove of garlic first). Pour over 600ml/1 pint/2½ cups semi-skimmed (low-fat) milk. Cover with foil and bake in a preheated oven at 180°C/350°F/Gas 4 for 40 minutes. Remove the foil and push the turnips down into the milk with the back of a spoon. Sprinkle the top with 25g/1oz/¼ cup grated Gruyère and bake for a further 30–40 minutes or the top is well-browned and the turnip very tender. Leave to stand for 5 minutes to let the turnip soak up more of the milk before serving.

NUTRITIONAL NOTES
Turnips and swedes are among the richest sources of folates. They also contain glucosinolates and other sulphur compounds which may lower the risk of cancer. A 100g/3½oz portion provides 28 calories and contains more than a third of the recommended daily intake of vitamin C.

Cabbages

While spiralizing cabbage doesn't produce noodles, it is a quick, easy and safe way to create fine even slices, ideal for using raw in salads and coleslaw or for boiling, steaming or braising.

Cabbage is probably the oldest cultivated vegetable, brought from Asia to northern Europe where it thrived in the cold coastal winds and was a vital food source during the long winter months. It became a popular vegetable in Eastern Europe and still features prominently in their cuisine. There are several varieties with different cropping times, such as the loose-leafed 'spring' cabbage and the 'winter' cabbages, including dark green crinkly-leaved Savoy, hard white 'Dutch' cabbage, popular for making coleslaw and sauerkraut, and red cabbage which is often pickled in spiced vinegar. It is these latter tight-hearted cabbages which can be successfully spiralized and are delicious when lightly cooked until barely tender, or slowly oven-baked.

BUYING AND STORING

For successful slicing on a spiralizer, it is better to choose a small tight-packed cabbage; the size depends on your spiralizer; most horizontal spiralizers have room for vegetables as long or wide as 20cm/8in, but some vertical spiralizers can only accommodate vegetables of half this length. Cabbage leaves should be firm and unblemished and if buying a Savoy cabbage, pick one with a few

How to spiralize

1 Remove any loose outer leaves; these can be kept for another recipe. Check and make sure that the remaining cabbage is clean and wash under cold running water if necessary.

2 Chop the base (stalk end) off the cabbage, cutting as cleanly and straight as possible.

3 Slot the spiralizer slicing blade into position and securely centre the cabbage on the spiralizer with the stalk end closest to the blade. Turn the handle continuously in a clockwise direction to create thin shreds of cabbage. Discard the left-over piece of cabbage.

ABOVE: A squeeze of fresh lemon juice improves the flavour of stir-fried cabbage.

ABOVE: Red cabbage will colour any dish with an attractive deep purple hue, it is good raw and cooked.

outer leaves still in place as these are good indicators of freshness. Winter cabbages will keep for a week or more in a cool place or in the salad drawer of the refrigerator; place in a plastic bag, but leave the top open. This helps prevent moisture loss, but still allows air to circulate.

HOW TO SERVE

Raw: A good addition to salads, raw cabbage works well with mustardy or nut oil-based vinaigrettes. Add them to the dressing an hour or so ahead of serving to soften and mellow their flavour, then add salad leaves just before serving. Finely shredded raw cabbage, either white or red, is the main ingredient of classic coleslaw; mix with mayonnaise or a lighter combination of yogurt and mayonnaise flavoured with a little lemon juice.

Steam-simmer: Boiling cabbage in lots of water should be avoided as nutrients will leach out (the aroma of boiled cabbage isn't too pleasant either). Instead, rinse the shredded cabbage in a colander under cold running water, then cook in a tightly covered pan over a low heat for 7–9 minutes or until tender; there will be enough water clinging to the cabbage to create a steamy atmosphere, but you can add a little butter or coconut oil to the base of the pan, if you like. Red cabbage takes a minute or two longer to cook than white or green cabbages.

Stir-fry: Heat 5ml/1 tsp coconut or sunflower oil in a large non-stick frying pan, skillet or wok. Add the cabbage and stir-fry for a minute, then add 30ml/2 tbsp vegetable stock or water, cover the pan with a lid and cook for a further 2 minutes. Remove the lid and continue to stir-fry for 1–2 minutes or until the cabbage is tender-crisp and the liquid has evaporated. Add a splash of lemon juice, a sprinkling of Chinese five-spice powder or some aniseedy flavours such as caraway seeds or chopped fresh tarragon.

NUTRITIONAL NOTES

Rich in phytonutrient antioxidants, this leafy vegetable is a great source of vitamins C and K, which plays an important role in bone health. It also contains moderate amounts of B-vitamins and many minerals including iron, potassium and magnesium. It is low in fat and has just 25 calories per 100g/3½oz.

Chayotes

Native to Mexico and central America, the chayote is cultivated in warm climates world-wide. Although technically a fruit, it is always eaten as a vegetable and may also be known as chouchoute or chuchu in Brazil and christophene or mirliton in Creole and Cajun cooking. Shaped like a pear, it has pale lime-green coloured skin, usually with a few deep vertical creases, a slightly watery dense texture and delicate flavour, somewhat like a cross between an apple and a cucumber, which allows it to absorb the flavour of any sauce or dressing it is served with. It has a large soft white stone or pit in the middle that is edible in younger chayotes, so it is better to use a horizontal spiralizer when preparing as this will remove most of the stone. Chayotes can be eaten with or without the skin when cooked, but should be peeled when served raw as the skin contains a sticky sap that some may find mildly irritating (this completely disappears when the chayote is cooked). For this reason, either peel under running water or wear gloves.

BUYING AND STORING
Sold in some supermarkets and Asian stores, the fruit should be bought when firm or just yielding to gentle pressure. Avoid any which are soft or beginning to shrivel. Store in a paper bag in the vegetable drawer of the refrigerator, but remember that they can over-ripen quickly, so use within a few days of purchase.

How to spiralize

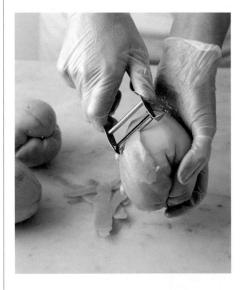

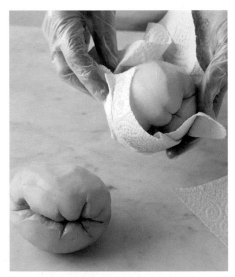

1 Thinly peel away the skin with a vegetable peeler if serving raw (ideally wear thin plastic or rubber gloves when preparing).

2 If you are cooking the chayote, rinse under running water and pat the skin dry with kitchen paper. Slot your chosen blade into position; chayote can be cut into any sized noodle or concertina slices if preferred.

3 Securely centre the fruit on the spiralizer, placing the thinner end at the front nearest to the blade, so the spikes can grip the wider end more firmly. Turn the handle continuously in a clockwise direction to create chayote noodles or slices. Discard the left-over piece of chayote.

HOW TO SERVE

Raw: Very thin (1mm/⅟₃₂in), thin (2mm/⅟₁₂in) and medium (3mm/⅛in) chayote noodles or slices are perfect served in salads. Toss in a simple vinaigrette dressing: whisk 60ml/4 tbsp light olive or sunflower oil with 15ml/1 tbsp sherry or white wine vinegar, salt and pepper and leave to marinate for 2–24 hours. Some of the juices from the chayote will dilute the dressing, so drain before serving. Chayote works well with ingredients such as avocados, fresh chillies and cooked beans, peas and lentils.

Boil: Drop the noodles into boiling lightly salted water and bring back to the boil. Simmer for 3–4 minutes until tender, but retaining the crisp texture. Drain well.

Sauté: Heat a little coconut or sunflower oil in a large non-stick frying pan or wok. Add the spiralized chayote and cook for 3–4 minutes, stirring frequently. Season with salt and pepper and a pinch of dried chillies.

Keep-it: Spiralized chayote can be kept for up to 24 hours in a plastic bag or airtight container in the refrigerator.

NUTRITIONAL NOTES
At just 16 calories per 100g/3½oz, chayote is very low in calories and contains no fat or cholesterol. It is a rich source of antioxidants, especially vitamin C and provides moderate amounts of potassium, and B-vitamins.

Plantains

Although plantain is a fruit, it is more often used as a vegetable, especially in South American, Caribbean and Asian cookery where it features in spicy meat and vegetarian dishes. Always cooked, it looks similar to a large banana, but with a much starchier texture and milder flavour. Like bananas, the skin colour changes from green to yellow and evenly black, becoming slightly sweeter as the fruit ripens. Keep plantains in a cool place, but avoid storing in the refrigerator.

TO SPIRALIZE

1 Both green and yellow plantains can be spiralized into noodles or slices; a vertical spiralizer is preferable for this as a horizontal one will remove a pencil-sized core from the middle which will be wasted. Choose the straightest 'fattest' fruit you can find, trim the ends straight and peel off the thick skin. Cut the plantain into two shorter lengths if it will not fit into the spiralizer whole.

2 Slot your chosen blade into position, then securely centre the plantain on the spiralizer and turn the handle in a clockwise direction to create plantain noodles or slices. These can be cut into shorter, more manageable lengths, using clean kitchen scissors.

3 To make plantain 'rice', process the noodles in a food processor using the pulse button, until the noodles are chopped into shorter pieces.

NUTRITIONAL NOTES
Plantains contain a large amount of starchy carbohydrate and have more calories weight for weight than ordinary bananas; 100g/3½oz provides 122 calories. They are a good source of vitamin C (although some of this will be destroyed in cooking), A and B-group vitamins, notably B6 (pyridoxine) plus potassium and adequate levels of iron, magnesium and phosphorous.

Aubergines (eggplants)

Aubergines can be tricky to spiralize as their texture is fairly soft and they have many tiny edible seeds. Providing you use a really firm one, it is possible to make both noodles and concertina-like slices, but these will be soft and not well-suited to cooking methods such as boiling or steaming as they tend to lose their shape and fall apart. They can however, be successfully stir-fried or baked and although their flavour is quite bland, this can be advantageous, as aubergines absorb flavourings and spices well, making them extremely versatile. Popular in Greek and Turkish cooking, they are an essential ingredient of moussaka and ratatouille and have a particular affinity with tomato-based sauces.

Aubergines come in several shapes and sizes, but the most common is the very deep purple-coloured variety with a cylindrical shape and rounded base. You may also find beautifully striped versions in the supermarket with paler purple skins, streaked with cream and occasionally small round yellow and green ones and white aubergines the size and shape of a very large egg; this variety inspired the name 'eggplant'. Some recipes may suggest salting aubergines after preparation. This draws out some of the moisture, so that they

OPPOSITE: Aubergines come in a variety of shapes and sizes. The best ones for spiralizing are long and straight; most familiar are the dark purple type but there are also lovely striped varieties.

How to spiralize

1 Rinse and pat dry, then slice off both ends, cutting as straight and evenly as possible. If necessary, peel back the stalk a little, so that you can get a clean cut. Cut the aubergine in half to make two shorter pieces, or if it will still be too long to fit your spiralizer, cut into three pieces (check carefully before cutting, as the fewer pieces, the less wastage there will be).

2 Slot your chosen blade into position. Securely centre the aubergine piece on the spiralizer and turn the handle continuously in a clockwise direction to create aubergine noodles or ribbons. These can be cut into shorter, more manageable lengths if you like, using clean kitchen scissors.

NUTRITIONAL NOTES

Aubergines have just 24 calories per 100g/3½oz. They are an excellent source of vitamin C and moderate amounts of B-vitamins, iron, potassium and calcium. They also contain bioflavonoids which may reduce the risk of strokes and certain cancers.

absorb a little less oil when frying, but was once done as a way of removing any bitter juices. Modern aubergines have been bred which are no longer bitter, making salting unnecessary. To prepare aubergines, rinse under cold water and pat dry, then slice off both ends with a sharp knife. There's no need to peel them, the skins are tender and will add colour to your dish (and peeled aubergines are almost impossible to spiralize).

BUYING AND STORING

When selecting aubergines for spiralizing, it is essential that they are really firm and fresh with a bright shiny skin and no wrinkles or brown patches. Small to medium-sized aubergines will have a sweeter flavour. The stalk end should be green and look fresh. After buying, store in the salad drawer of the refrigerator for up to 5 days.

HOW TO SERVE

Stir-fry: This is probably the best way to cook spiralized aubergine, as some of the water content will evaporate as you cook. Use a good quality large non-stick frying pan, skillet or wok. Add 15ml/1 tbsp olive oil for every spiralized medium aubergine and heat until very hot, as this will brown some of the pieces and add a delicious smoky flavour. Add the aubergine and cook over a high heat for a minute or two, then lower the heat and continue cooking for 2–3 minutes for noodles and 3–4 minutes for slices, stirring frequently, until cooked to your liking. Don't be tempted to add more oil to the pan, although the aubergine noodles will have soaked up the oil immediately and look impossibly dry. As they continue to cook, the aubergine will start to produce a little juice and stop them sticking to the pan. If they do start to catch, add a teaspoon or two of water and continue cooking until this has evaporated. Add seasoning at the beginning of cooking or a crushed clove of garlic halfway through.

Roast: Drizzle spiralized aubergines with 15ml–30ml/1–2 tbsp olive oil in a roasting pan. Toss together to lightly coat in oil and spread out into an even layer. Roast at 200°C/400°F/Gas 6 for 20–25 minutes, turning a couple of times towards the end of cooking time to ensure they cook evenly.

Apples and pears

Most ripe fruit is either too soft or too juicy to be successfully spiralized, but apples and pears can both be cut into noodles of different thicknesses, concertina-type ribbons or fine even slices. Spiralized, they can be used raw or cooked and although they usually feature in sweet recipes, they also work well in savoury dishes including salads and soups, and have a particular affinity with vegetables like cabbage and kohlrabi and with meat such as pork. Warm spices including cinnamon, cloves and ginger complement the fruit.

While there are thousands of varieties of apples and pears, the choice in greengrocers and supermarkets tends to be limited to just a few. Some of the most popular eating apple varieties you'll find in the shops are Cox's orange pippin, Gala, Braeburn, Granny Smith and Golden Delicious. Farmer's markets often offer a wider choice of lesser known types. Cooking apples include Bramley Seedling which are larger than eating apples, with thicker vibrant green-coloured skins and tart-tasting flesh. They are great for baking, but although they can be spiralized for quick preparation (you should peel them first), they will not hold their shape when cooked. This may be advantageous if you are making an apple sauce, but not so good if you are looking for attractive apple noodles. Cooking apples are never served raw and need copious amounts of sugar to sweeten them to most people's taste.

Like apples, some types of pear are better eaten raw, others, such as Packham are better cooked, but most varieties of pear can be used for either purpose. Favourites include brown and green speckled Conference pears, Williams, which has a thin yellow skin and Comice, with a pale yellow skin with a green tinge often blushed with red.

BUYING AND STORING

When buying apples, choose firm fruit without any bruises, wrinkles, or obvious damage. Organic apples may look less attractive, but often have a better flavour, although you should try to choose evenly round fruit as they will spiralize better. Pears should be firm and plump and just slightly under-ripe as they can ripen in a day or two and then pass their peak very quickly and develop a 'woolly' texture. You should be able to smell when a pear is ripe or you can gently feel around the base of the stalk where it should give slightly when gently pressed; the rest of the pear should still feel fairly firm. Short squat pears such as Comice are easier to spiralize than more tapering varieties such as Conference and the resulting noodles tend to be more attractive as the skins are prettily coloured and the flesh whiter.

Store both apples and pears in a cool place, away from direct sunlight; the salad drawer of the refrigerator is a good place to store them if you are planning to keep for longer than a few days as it will keep them fresher and firmer.

HOW TO SERVE

Raw: Apples and pears are often served raw in recipes, especially breakfast and salad dishes.

Cooked: Cook noodles and ribbons over a moderate heat for about 3 minutes until tender, preferably in a non-stick pan. You can either use a small knob of butter, coconut oil or a spoonful of fruit juice or water to start the cooking process and to stop the fruit from sticking to the pan or burning. Cover the pan with a lid after the first minute so that the fruit will steam in its own juices.

NUTRITIONAL NOTES

Apples and pears have a high water content, but both are a useful source of vitamin C, although this is reduced if cooked. They also contain good amounts of potassium, pectin and fibre which can be valuable in lowering harmful LDL cholesterol levels in the body.

How to spiralize

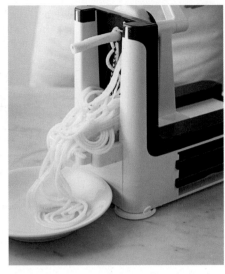

1 A horizontal spiralizer is preferable when spiralizing apples and pears as it will remove some of the core; this is particularly useful for non-organic fruit as any remnants of insecticide collect in the core and pips. If you are using a vertical spiralizer, remove pieces of core and any pips as you spiralize. Unless the skin of the fruit is tough or very blemished, leave both apples and pears unpeeled.

2 Wash thoroughly and dry with a clean dish towel or kitchen paper. Remove the stems, then slot your chosen blade into position. Securely centre the fruit on the spiralizer with the stem end of the fruit nearest to the blade and turn the handle continuously in a clockwise direction to create noodles, ribbons or slices.

3 Cut the noodles or ribbons into more manageable lengths if you like, using clean kitchen scissors. Both apple and pears will discolour quickly when cut, so toss in lemon or orange juice or use promptly in the recipe as instructed.

BELOW: Apples are ideal firm fruits for spiralizing into slices.

BELOW: Apples also spiralize easily into very thin noodles.

BELOW: Spiralize unpeeled pears into thin noodles for an attractive garnish.

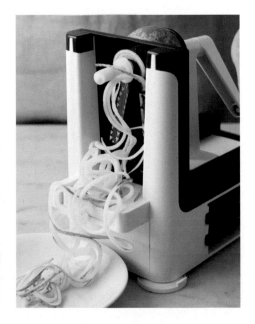

Using left-overs: stock and soup

A spiralizer is an economical way of preparing all types of vegetables and fruit. Producing a big bowlful of noodles from just a couple of courgettes or dozens of beautifully thin slices from a single potato really makes the most of your ingredients. However, no matter what type of spiralizer you use, you are always left with a small piece of vegetable. There's no need to throw this away, as it can be used to make fantastically flavoured vegetable stock or a simple soup, as shown here. If you spiralize a lot of vegetables, save the left-over pieces in a plastic bag in the refrigerator, where they will keep for 3–4 days until you are ready to use them in one go, or if you spiralize less often, roughly chop the pieces of left-over vegetables and keep in a bag in the freezer, adding to it for several weeks.

Basic vegetable stock

Makes about 600ml/1 pint/2½ cups
15ml/1 tbsp olive oil
150g/5oz (or more) left-over pieces of onion, carrot and fennel
150g/5oz (or more) left-over pieces of courgette (zucchini), butternut squash, (bell) pepper, kohlrabi, parsnip, swede (rutagaba) and turnip
Any other left-over pieces of vegetables such as celery, leeks, parsley stalks and a few pieces of brown or Spanish (Bermuda) onion skin (these add a lovely golden colour)
1 bay leaf
5 black peppercorns
750ml/1¼ pints/3 cups cold water

Store left-over bits of onion, carrots and fennel in one bag or airtight container, and left-over bits of courgettes (zucchini), butternut squash, (bell) peppers, kohlrabi, cabbage, swede (rutabaga) and turnip in another. You don't need to include all the vegetables listed, but try to use several different varieties and only add small amounts of cabbage, parsnip, swede or turnip as these can overpower the flavour. Beetroot (beet), cucumber, chayote, mooli (daikon) and potatoes aren't suitable for making stock.

1 Heat the oil in a large pan, add the onion, carrot and fennel and sauté over a moderately low heat for 3–4 minutes or until the onion pieces just start to colour (don't over-cook or the stock will be bitter).
2 Add all the other ingredients and slowly bring to the boil on the lowest possible heat. Once the stock starts to simmer, cook for a further 15 minutes, then turn off the heat, cover the pan and leave for 15 minutes.
3 Strain the stock through a fine sieve or strainer and discard the vegetables, bay leaf and peppercorns. The stock is ready to be used or can be left to cool and stored in the refrigerator for up to 3 days, or frozen in batches for future use.

Cook's tip
If you want small amounts of vegetable stock for sauces and gravies, freeze some of the stock in ice cube trays.

Simple vegetable soup

All types of vegetable spiralizer left-overs can be used for this healthy low-fat soup, except cucumber. If you don't have a lot of left-over pieces of onion from spiralizing, add an extra onion at the start of cooking to ensure the soup is well-flavoured. Other seasonings can be added to the soup either during or after cooking.

1 Heat the oil, butter or margarine in a large pan and cook the onion and garlic over a low heat for 6–7 minutes or until softened. Stir in the left-over spiralized vegetable pieces.

2 Pour in 500ml/17fl oz/generous 2 cups of liquid and add the aromatics and seasoning. Bring to the boil, lower the heat to a gentle simmer, cover the pan and cook for 15 minutes or until the vegetables are tender. If you are using lentils as a thickener, add with the vegetables.

3 Leave to cool in the pan for 10 minutes, then remove the bay leaf, if used, and purée the soup with a hand-held liquidizer or in a blender. If using pastina as a thickener, add after the soup has been puréed and cook for a further 3–4 minutes or until tender.

4 Reheat the soup until piping hot, adding the remaining liquid if you want a thinner consistency, or you could add dairy or soya milk if you prefer. Serve in warm bowls and add a swirl of yogurt and a scattering of fresh chopped herbs, if liked.

Serves 3–4

For the base ingredients:
15ml/1 tbsp olive or sunflower oil or 15g/½oz butter or margarine
1 small onion, sliced using the spiralizer slicing blade
1 garlic clove, crushed

For the main ingredients:
225g/8oz left-over spiralized vegetable pieces (fresh or frozen)

For the liquid:
500–600ml/17fl oz–1 pint/generous 2–2½ cups stock, vegetable cooking water or water

For the aromatics:
1 bay leaf and/or 5ml/1 tsp dried mixed herbs, or pinch dried chilli flakes or 5–10ml/1–2 tsp curry paste
salt and ground black pepper

For the thickeners (optional):
50g/2oz/⅓ cup red lentils or pastina (tiny soup pasta), soaked in 150ml/ ¼ pint/⅔ cup boiling water for 10 minutes and drained

BREAKFASTS & BRUNCHES

Healthy fresh fruit and vegetables are the best way to start the day and using a spiralizer will help you prepare them in minutes. Enjoy a delicious bowl of chia porridge or Bircher muesli on a weekday, or some indulgent plantain pancakes or tempting oat and apple muffins, still warm from the oven, for a weekend brunch when there's more time. You'll find well-known classics here with a new twist, such as eggs Benedict, served on a bed of sweet potato noodles, and smoked trout kedgeree with spiralized celeriac rice. And when you want a portable breakfast, try protein-packed fruit and seed breakfast bars to keep you sustained until lunchtime.

Spiralized plaintain pancakes

Serves 4–6 (makes about 12 pancakes)

115g/4oz/1 cup self-raising (self-rising) flour

115g/4oz/1 cup self-raising (self-rising) wholemeal (whole-wheat) flour

Pinch of salt

30ml/2 tbsp light muscovado (brown) sugar

1 large plantain

2 medium eggs, separated

350ml/12fl oz/1½ cups dairy or plant milk such as soya or almond milk

Coconut or sunflower oil, to fry

Thick natural (plain) yogurt, honey, agave or maple syrup, to serve

1 Sift the flours and salt into a bowl, adding the bran left in the sieve or strainer. Stir in the muscovado sugar, breaking up any lumps.

2 Spiralize the plantain into thin (2mm/¹⁄₁₂in) noodles, then cut into shorter lengths, roughly 5cm/2in long. Add to the dry ingredients, separating the strands with your fingertips, so that they don't clump together.

3 Mix the egg yolks and milk in a jug or pitcher. Add to the dry ingredients and whisk together to make a smooth thick batter. Whisk the egg whites in a clean bowl until they form soft peaks. Stir a large spoonful into the batter to loosen it a little, then gently fold in the remainder with a large metal spoon.

4 Heat a griddle or large non-stick frying pan over a moderate heat, then lightly grease with oil. Drop large spoonfuls of the batter into the pan, spacing them well-apart. You should be able to cook 3 or 4 pancakes at a time.

5 Cook for 2–3 minutes or until dark golden on the underside and tiny bubbles appear on the surface. Turn over and cook for another 2–3 minutes. Remove from the pan and keep warm in a low oven while cooking the rest of the pancakes, adding a little more oil when needed. Serve warm with yogurt and honey or syrup drizzled over the top.

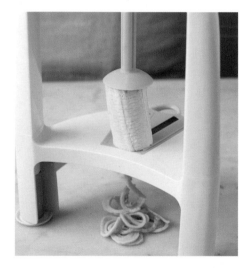

These light and fluffy little pancakes contain starchy plantain, which has a subtle banana-like flavour. Spiralizing rather than simply slicing will ensure it is cut finely enough to cook through in the relatively short frying time.

These muffins contain oats soaked in vanilla-flavoured milk together with spices and spiralized apples. Measure out the dry ingredients the night before, so that you can make and bake these in the morning in less than half an hour.

Oat and apple breakfast muffins

1 Preheat the oven to 200°C/400°F/Gas 6. Put the oats in a bowl and pour over the milk and vanilla extract. Stir, then leave to soak for a few minutes. Lightly grease a 9-hole muffin or deep bun tin or pan with oil. Alternatively line with paper muffin cases.

2 Mix the flours, baking powder, cinnamon, salt and sugar in a large bowl. Spiralize the apples into medium (3mm/⅛in) noodles, leaving the skins on and discarding the core, then roughly chop into shorter lengths, about 5cm/2in.

3 Stir the spiralized apples into the dry ingredients and make a well in the middle. Stir the oil and egg into the soaked oat mixture. Add the oat mixture all at once to the dry ingredients and mix briefly until just combined. Do not overmix.

4 Spoon the batter into the prepared muffin cups, dividing it evenly. Bake in the oven for 18–20 minutes, or until risen and golden. Cool in the tin for 5 minutes, then turn out on to a wire rack. Serve warm.

Cook's tip
You can also make these muffins substituting 2 medium spiralized carrots for the apples. Add a few chopped nuts if liked, for extra protein and minerals.

  (if using non-dairy milk)

Makes 9
50g/2oz/scant ½ cup rolled oats
250ml/8fl oz/1 cup milk (dairy or plant milk such as soya or almond milk)
10ml/2 tsp vanilla extract
115g/4oz/1 cup self-raising (self-rising) wholemeal (whole-wheat) flour
150g/5oz/1¼ cups self-raising (self-rising) flour, preferably unbleached
7.5ml/1½ tsp baking powder
10ml/2 tsp ground cinnamon
2.5ml/½ tsp salt
90g/3½oz/7 tbsp light muscovado (brown) or coconut sugar
2 medium eating apples
105ml/7 tbsp melted and cooled coconut oil or sunflower oil
1 egg, lightly beaten

Naturally sweet and moist, these chewy protein-packed bars are ideal for days when you are short of time and want a portable breakfast or if you aren't keen to eat much in the morning, as they also make a great mid-morning snack when you need a long-lasting energy boost.

Spiralized fruit and seed breakfast bars

Makes 10–12
30ml/2 tbsp sunflower seeds
30ml/2 tbsp pumpkin seeds
75g/3oz coconut oil, butter or
   baking margarine
45ml/3 tbsp agave syrup
2 medium firm ripe pears
2 ripe bananas, about 300g/11oz
   (weighed with their skins on),
   peeled and mashed
90g/3½oz/1 cup rolled oats
75g/3oz/¾ cup millet flakes
30ml/2 tbsp sesame seeds
30ml/2 tbsp desiccated (dry
   unsweetened shredded) coconut
10ml/2 tsp ground ginger
Pinch of salt (optional)

1 Preheat the oven to 180°C/350°F/Gas 4. Line a 28 x 18cm/11 x 7in baking tin or pan with baking parchment. Roughly chop the sunflower and pumpkin seeds into smaller pieces.

2 Put the coconut oil, butter or margarine and agave syrup in a medium pan. Spiralize the pears, peeled if preferred, with the medium (3mm/⅛in) noodle blade, then cut into slightly shorter lengths. Add to the pan and gently heat, stirring occasionally until the coconut oil, butter or margarine has melted and everything is combined. Stir in the mashed bananas.

3 Put the oats, millet flakes, sesame seeds, desiccated coconut, ginger and salt, if using, in a large bowl and stir together. Add the pear and banana mixture and mix thoroughly.

4 Spoon the mixture into the prepared tin and spread out evenly. Bake for 30 minutes, or until dark golden brown. Remove from the oven and leave for 5 minutes, then mark into 10–12 bars. Cool completely in the tin. Turn out and store in a cool place in an airtight container. In warm weather keep the breakfast bars in the refrigerator.

Cook's tip
Wrap and freeze the bars individually; they'll defrost at room temperature in about 20 minutes. Alternatively, add a frozen bar to your lunch box in the morning; it will help keep the rest of your lunch cool.

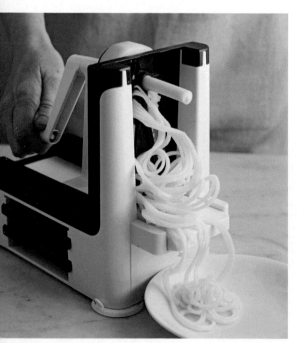

This version is similar to the original recipe of a nutritious raw breakfast which was created by Swiss physician Dr. Bircher-Brenner over a century ago. As he discovered, soaking the cereal makes it easier to digest and freshly spiralized apples add both vitamins and fibre.

Bircher muesli spiralizer-style

   VT **V** **DF** (if using non-dairy milk & yogurt)

Serves 4

115g/4oz/generous 1 cup rolled oats
250ml/8fl oz/1 cup semi-skimmed (low-fat) or plant-based milk eg soya or almond milk
60ml/4 tbsp apple juice
2 medium eating apples
10ml/2 tsp lemon juice
50g/2oz/½ cup toasted hazelnuts, roughly chopped
150ml/¼ pint/⅔ cup low-fat bio yogurt or soya yogurt
20ml/4 tsp clear honey, maple or agave syrup

1 Put the oats in a medium bowl and pour over the milk and apple juice. Stir, then cover and leave to soak overnight in the refrigerator.

2 The next day, spiralize the apples into thin (2mm/1/12in) or medium (3mm/1/8in) noodles, leaving the skins on, if you prefer, and discarding the core. Cut into shorter lengths and toss with the lemon juice to prevent browning.

3 Stir the apples, hazelnuts and half of the yogurt into the soaked oat mixture, then spoon the muesli into bowls. Top each with a spoonful of the remaining yogurt and a drizzle of honey or syrup before serving.

Cook's tip
Use your favourite combination of fresh fruit, toasted nuts or coconut to serve with the muesli. You can also soak dried fruit such as raisins or chopped apricots, adding an extra spoonful or two of milk. Apple juice is a traditional addition to Bircher muesli, but you can replace it with milk if preferred.

Chia porridge with spiralized pear

1 Put the chia seeds in a bowl and pour over the milk. Leave for a few minutes, then stir well, cover and leave in the refrigerator overnight.

2 The next day, spiralize the pear with the medium (3mm/⅛in) noodle blade, leaving the skin on and discarding the cores. Cut the noodles into shorter manageable lengths, then stir into the soaked chia mixture. Spoon into bowls and serve straight away.

Cook's tip
Choose a well-flavoured just-ripe pear for this breakfast dish; one with a blushed rosy skin such as a red Bartlett or red Williams will add a hint of colour.

This tiny grain is exceptionally nutritious and soaks up huge amounts of liquid, needing no further cooking

V   DF   GF   P   VT

Serves 2
75g/3oz/⅓ cup chia seeds
475ml/16fl oz/2 cups almond or
　coconut milk
1 large ripe pear

With a wealth of antioxidants, minerals and omega-3 and a complete source of protein, chia seeds make an energizing start to the day. Overnight soaking allows the seeds to expand. Strands of juicy spiralized pear complement the nutty flavour perfectly.

Created as a brunch dish at New York's Delmonico's restaurant, this is traditionally served on a buttered toasted English muffin with prosciutto and topped with high-fat hollandaise sauce. Spiralized sweet potato makes a delicious alternative to the bread and here the fat and calorie content of the hollandaise is reduced by using Greek yogurt.

Eggs Benedict with spiralized sweet potato

1 For the sauce, whisk together the egg yolks, mustard, yogurt, salt and white pepper in a small heatproof bowl over a pan of barely simmering water. Cook for 10–12 minutes, stirring constantly. The sauce will become thinner initially as the yogurt warms, but will then start to thicken. Turn off the heat, leaving the bowl over the hot water to keep it warm.

2 Half-fill a pan with water, add the vinegar and a pinch of salt and bring to the boil. Spiralize the sweet potato with the medium (3mm/⅛in) noodle blade. Heat the oil in a large non-stick frying pan, add the sweet potato and stir-fry over a moderate heat for 2 minutes. Add the stock, cover the pan with the lid and cook for a further 2 minutes or until the sweet potatoes are tender and cooked through.

3 Reduce the heat of the pan of boiling water and vinegar, so that it is barely simmering. Break each egg into a cup, then slide it carefully into the water. Gently turn the white around the egg with a spoon. Cook for 3–4 minutes until the white is set.

4 Add the prosciutto and spinach to the pan of spiralized sweet potato and stir. Re-cover and cook for a further minute or two, or until the spinach is just wilted and the sweet potato is tender. Turn off the heat.

5 Remove the eggs from the pan, one at a time, using a slotted spoon, and drain on kitchen paper. If liked, cut off any ragged edges with kitchen scissors.

6 Divide the noodles, prosciutto and spinach mixture between warmed plates and top each with a poached egg. Spoon the warm yogurt hollandaise sauce over the egg and serve straight away, with ground black pepper if liked.

GF

Serves 4
5ml/1 tsp vinegar
Pinch of salt
1 large sweet potato, about 350g/
    12oz, peeled
10ml/2 tsp olive oil
60ml/4 tbsp vegetable stock
4 eggs
4 slices prosciutto, about 50g/2oz,
    trimmed of fat and cut into
    1cm/½in strips
25g/1oz baby spinach leaves
Ground black pepper (optional)

For the yogurt hollandaise:
2 egg yolks
5ml/1 tsp Dijon mustard
150ml/¼ pint/⅔ cup Greek (US strained
    plain) yogurt
Salt and ground white pepper

A combination of spiralized butternut squash and fine yellow cornmeal gives this cornbread a wonderful texture and vibrant golden colour. It's made with buttermilk, which unlike its name suggests is very low in fat. A delicious accompaniment to crispy bacon or softly cooked eggs, serve while still warm and fresh from the oven.

Spiralized squash and buttermilk brunch bread

Makes 6–8 portions
200g/7oz butternut squash, peeled
250ml/8fl oz/1 cup buttermilk
40g/1½oz/3 tbsp coconut oil, butter
   or margarine
30ml/2 tbsp honey
115g/4oz/⅔ cup fine yellow cornmeal,
   preferably stoneground
115g/4oz/1 cup plain (all-purpose) flour,
   preferably unbleached
7.5ml/1½ tsp baking powder
2.5ml/½ tsp bicarbonate of soda
   (baking soda)
2.5ml/½ tsp salt
1 egg, lightly beaten

Spiralize the butternut squash the night before and you can make this simple soda bread in less than half an hour

1 Preheat the oven to 200°C/400°F/Gas 6. Line a 20cm/8in round cake tin or pan with baking parchment and lightly grease.

2 Spiralize the butternut squash with the medium (3mm/⅛in) noodle blade, then cut into shorter lengths, roughly 5cm/2in long. Place in a pan and pour over the buttermilk. Add the coconut oil, butter or margarine and honey. Gently heat, stirring occasionally until the fat has just melted. Turn off the heat.

3 Put the cornmeal, flour, baking powder, bicarbonate of soda and salt into a large bowl and mix together. Make a hollow in the middle. Add the egg and pour in the warm milk and butternut squash mixture. Stir together to make a smooth thick batter.

4 Pour and scrape the mixture into the prepared tin and spread evenly. Bake for 15–20 minutes or until golden and a cocktail stick (toothpick) inserted into the middle comes out clean. Leave in the tin for 5 minutes, then turn out and cut into wedges. Serve warm.

Cook's tips
Cornbread is best eaten on the same day. It can be frozen for up to a month, then allowed to defrost and gently warmed before serving. If you can't find buttermilk, stir 15ml/1 tbsp lemon juice into 350ml/12fl oz/1½ cups semi-skimmed (low-fat) milk or or plant-based milk eg soya or almond milk, less 15ml/1 tbsp, and leave to stand for 5 minutes before using. Alternatively, use a mixture of half natural (plain) yogurt and milk.

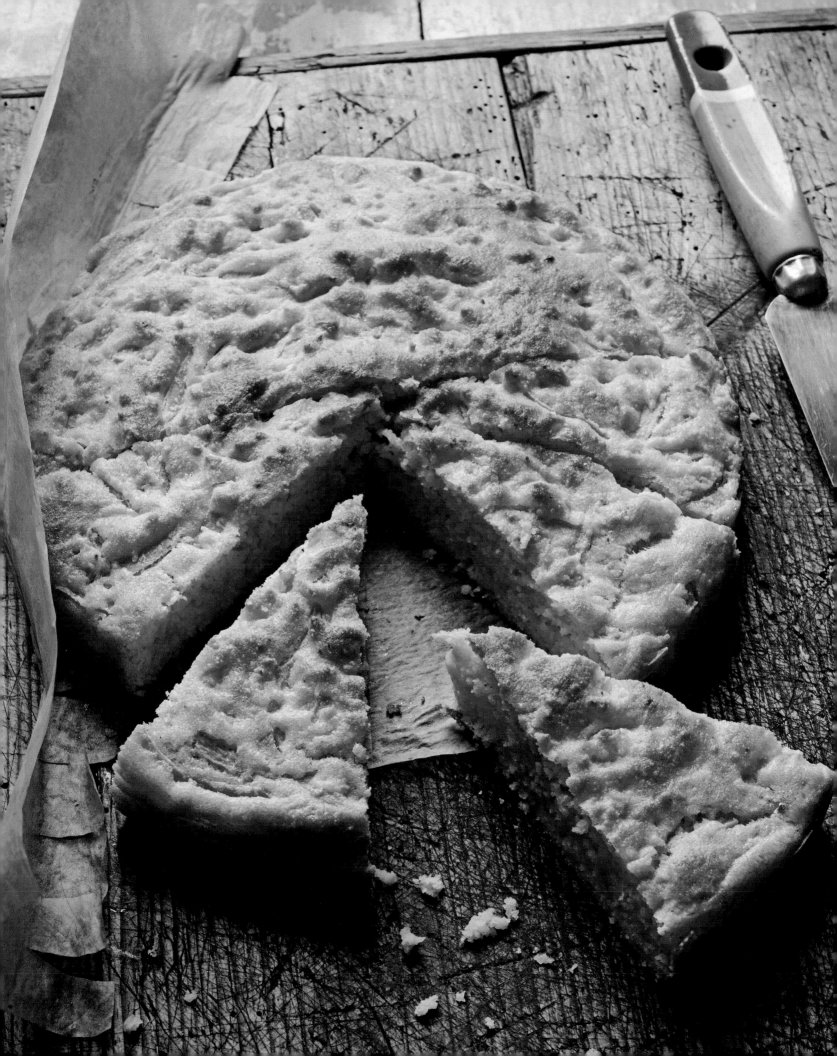

Tender pink smoked trout takes the place of the traditional smoked haddock in this lightly spiced brunch dish, and works well with the mild celery-like flavour of celeriac, which makes a low-carbohydrate alternative to rice. Hard-boiled quail's eggs can be fiddly and time-consuming to peel, so here they are fried until the yolks are softly set.

Smoked trout kedgeree with spiralized celeriac

1 Spiralize the celeriac using the medium (3mm/⅛in) noodle blade. Snip into slightly shorter lengths, then place in a food processor and pulse until the noodles look like rice (see page 27).

2 Heat 10ml/2 tsp of the oil in a medium pan and gently cook the onion for 6–7 minutes, stirring frequently until tender. Add the curry paste and stir over a low heat for a minute, then add the celeriac 'rice' and vegetable stock. Cover with a lid and cook for 5–6 minutes, stirring occasionally, until just tender. Remove the lid for the last minute or two of cooking time, to allow some of the juices to evaporate.

3 Meanwhile, heat the remaining 10ml/2 tsp oil in a non-stick frying pan and crack in the eggs. Cook for about 1 minute, or until they are cooked to your liking. Remove them from the pan in the order in which you have added them; the first should be cooked by the time you have added the last egg to the pan.

4 Stir the flaked trout, almonds and fresh coriander or parsley into the 'rice' and season to taste with salt and pepper. Gently heat for a further minute until the fish is warmed through. Serve straight away topped with the fried quail's eggs.

Cook's tip
You can buy ready-toasted almonds or toast your own by dry-frying in a non-stick pan over a moderate heat. Stir every few seconds and turn off the heat as soon as the almonds start to turn golden; they will continue cooking in the residual heat.

DF **GF**

Serves 4
1 large celeriac, weighing about 800g/1¾lb
20ml/4 tsp coconut or sunflower oil
1 small red onion, spiralized
15ml/1 tbsp korma curry paste
120ml/4fl oz/½ cup vegetable stock
8 quail's eggs
350g/12oz smoked trout fillets, skinned and boned and flaked into large pieces
50g/2oz/½ cup toasted flaked (sliced) almonds
30ml/2 tbsp chopped fresh coriander (cilantro) or parsley
Salt and ground black pepper

Don't just serve this high-protein, low-carbohydrate dish at the start of the day; it also makes a lovely light lunch or supper dish and is elegant enough for a casual dinner-party

SOUPS

Nothing matches the flavour of a good home-made soup and vegetables often play the starring role. Spiralizing reduces preparation time and makes soups look sensational. Whether you want to make a sophisticated appetizer, a light lunch or supper dish, or to create a warming one-bowl meal, you'll find plenty of choice here from Japanese-style ramens to paprika beef and spiralized vegetable soup with dumplings. And, while there's nothing more restorative in winter than a steaming bowl of soup, there's a recipe to suit even the warmest days with a classic chilled gazpacho.

Ramen is the name of a Japanese noodle soup dish. Although 'ramen' usually refers to the firm and slightly chewy wheat noodles, vegetable noodles are often used instead, to make a lighter, fresher dish. The soup relies on a well-flavoured but not overpowering stock for the clear broth base, either dashi or a simple mixed vegetable stock.

Miso ramen with spiralized mooli noodles

1 Cut the coarse green tops off the spring onions, then slice the rest finely on the diagonal and put to one side. Place the green tops in a large pan with the coriander stalks, fresh root ginger, star anise and dashi or vegetable stock.

2 Heat gently until boiling, then lower the heat and simmer for 10 minutes. Strain, reserving the stock. Blend half a ladleful of the hot stock with the miso paste in a small bowl and set aside. Return the stock to the pan and reheat until simmering.

3 Meanwhile, bring a pan of water to the boil and lower the eggs on a spoon into the simmering water. Heat the water until bubbling gently, then cook the eggs for 5–6 minutes. Remove the eggs and place in a bowl of cold water. When the eggs are just cool enough to handle, remove the shells and cut each egg in half lengthways; the whites should be very firm, but the yolks still slightly soft.

4 While the stock and eggs are cooking, spiralize the mooli using the thin, spaghetti-sized noodle blade. When the stock and eggs are ready, add the mooli noodles to the simmering stock, bring back to the boil and cook for 2 minutes or until just tender. Remove the mooli noodles and divide between warmed soup bowls, pushing the noodles to one side of the bowls.

5 Stir in the reserved stock and miso mixture into the rest of the stock, with soy sauce to taste. Add the tofu and quickly heat until warmed through. Leaving the stock on the heat, remove the tofu with a slotted spoon and divide the tofu between the bowls, placing next to the noodles.

6 Add the spring onions and red chilli, if using, to the stock, then ladle over the noodles and tofu. Arrange two egg halves on top of each and serve straight away, garnished with chopped fresh coriander leaves.

Cook's tips

Miso is a fermented paste made from soya beans and rice, barley, wheat or rye. It gives a deeply savoury intensity to this soup.

Dashi powder is available in most Asian stores and can be reconstituted to make dashi stock. Alternatively, you can make your own by gently simmering 10cm/4in kombu seaweed in 1.2 litres/2 pints/5 cups water for 10 minutes (do not boil rapidly or the dashi will be bitter). Add 15g/½oz dried bonito flakes for the last 2 minutes of cooking time. Strain the stock through a fine sieve or strainer.

VT **P** **DF**

Serves 4

6 spring onions (scallions)

15g/½oz fresh coriander (cilantro) stalks, plus extra leaves to garnish

3 thin slices fresh root ginger

1 star anise

1.2 litres/2 pints/5 cups dashi stock (see tips) or vegetable stock

30ml/2 tbsp miso paste

4 small eggs, at room temperature

1 large mooli (daikon)

15–30ml/1–2 tbsp Japanese soy sauce (shoyu)

350g/12oz firm tofu, cut into 2cm/¾in cubes

1 fresh red chilli, seeded and shredded (optional)

Delicate fresh pink salmon and the subtle flavour of spiralized courgette noodles make a great partnership in this Japanese-style soup. Crisp beansprouts and tender pak choi add both taste and texture, making it a light and healthy meal in a bowl.

Seared salmon ramen with spiralized courgettes

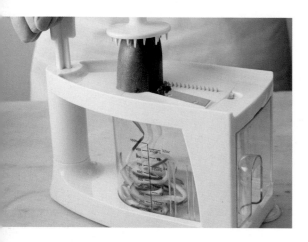

GF DF

Serves 4
1 litre/1¾ pints/4 cups vegetable stock
4 spring onions (scallions), thickly sliced
2cm/¾in piece fresh root ginger, sliced
2 star anise
30ml/2 tbsp soy sauce
30ml/2 tbsp sake (rice wine) or dry sherry
2 courgettes (zucchini)
2 small heads pak choi (bok choy)
400g/14oz salmon fillet
15ml/1 tbsp groundnut (peanut) oil
75g/3oz/⅓ cup beansprouts

1 Pour the stock into a large pan, add the spring onions, ginger and star anise and then bring to the boil. Cover and simmer for 15 minutes, then turn off the heat and leave to stand and infuse for a further 15 minutes. Remove the spring onions, ginger and star anise with a slotted spoon and discard. Add the soy sauce and sake or dry sherry.

2 Meanwhile, spiralize the courgettes using the fine (spaghetti-sized) noodle blade. Break up the pak choi and slice if thick. Cut the salmon into 1cm/½in thin slices on the diagonal.

3 Bring the flavoured stock back to the boil. Brush a ridged griddle, frying pan or skillet with the oil and heat.

4 Add the courgette noodles to the boiling stock and simmer for 2–3 minutes or until tender. Remove from the stock with a slotted spoon and using a fork, twist into four 'nests'. Place in warmed bowls.

5 Add the pak choi and beansprouts to the boiling stock and cook for 2 minutes. At the same time, sear the salmon slices in the griddle pan for 1–2 minutes on each side or until just cooked and marked with browned ridged lines.

6 Lift out the pak choi and beansprouts with a slotted spoon and place around the noodle nests. Arrange the salmon on top. Ladle the hot broth into the bowls and serve immediately.

Cook's tips
Chill the salmon in the freezer for about 10 minutes before slicing; it will be much easier to cut into thin slices. Coconut oil can be used instead of groundnut oil.

Most minestrone soup recipes are based on summer-grown vegetables such as courgettes and fresh tomatoes. This one is made with winter produce including root vegetables, potato and hearty Savoy cabbage, and everyday store cupboard ingredients such as beans and chopped canned tomatoes: it's simpler and quicker to make, but just as nutritious.

Spiralized winter vegetable minestrone

1 Spiralize the onion using the medium (3mm/⅛in) noodle blade, then cut into shorter lengths, about 5cm/2in. Heat the oil in a large pan. Add the onion, cover and cook for 4–5 minutes, stirring occasionally until it is almost soft.

2 Add the garlic and cook, stirring for a further minute, then add the thyme, bay leaf, chopped tomatoes, tomato purée and stock. Cover the pan with a lid and turn the heat to low.

3 Meanwhile, spiralize the carrot, swede, celeriac and potato using the medium (3mm/⅛in) noodle blade. Cut the spiralized vegetables into shorter lengths, about 5cm/2in. Add to the pan and bring to the boil, then simmer, covered, for 12 minutes.

4 Stir in the beans and shredded cabbage, or 15g/1oz spiralized cabbage. Cover and cook for a further 3–5 minutes, or until all the vegetables are tender.

5 Discard the thyme and bay leaf and season the soup to taste with salt and ground black pepper. Ladle into warmed soup bowls and serve.

Variation
For a summer version of this soup, replace the swede (rutabaga) with 2 spiralized courgettes (zucchini) and the celeriac with 2 sticks of celery, finely chopped. Stir in 30ml/2 tbsp green pesto at the end of cooking.

A wide variety of vegetables ensures that this simple soup is as healthy as it is delicious

VT GF DF V

Serves 6
1 onion, peeled
15ml/1 tbsp olive oil
2 cloves garlic, crushed
1 sprig of fresh thyme or 1.5ml/¼ tsp dried thyme
1 bay leaf
400g/14oz can chopped tomatoes
15ml/1 tbsp tomato purée (paste)
1.2 litres/2 pints/5 cups hot vegetable stock
1 large carrot, peeled
1 small swede (rutabaga), about 200g/7oz, peeled
1 small celeriac, about 400g/14oz, peeled
1 medium potato, about 200g/7oz, peeled
150g/5oz/1 cup cooked or canned borlotti or cannellini beans
1 large Savoy cabbage leaf, finely shredded
Salt and ground black pepper

Here, the slightly peppery flavour of kohlrabi is enhanced with a hint of sweet apple and ginger. Spiralizing is a quick way to prepare the kohlrabi and ensures it cooks in as little time as possible, retaining the delicate fresh flavour and maximizing the vitamin content.

Spiralized kohlrabi and apple soup

1 Slice the onion using the slicing blade on the spiralizer. Heat the oil in a large pan. Add the onion, cover and cook for 6–7 minutes, stirring occasionally until the onion is soft.

2 Add the garlic and ginger and cook, stirring for a further minute. Pour in the stock and leave on a low heat while preparing the kohlrabi and apple.

3 Spiralize the kohlrabi and apple using the medium (3mm/⅛in) noodle blade. Cut the noodles into shorter lengths about 4cm/1½in. Add to the pan, season with salt and pepper to taste, then bring to the boil.

4 Turn down the heat until the soup is gently simmering and cover the pan with a lid. Cook for 12–15 minutes, or until the kohlrabi is very tender. Purée about three-quarters of the soup in a blender or with a hand-held blender, until very smooth (if using a hand-held blender, ladle about a quarter of the spiralized vegetable soup into a small bowl).

5 Stir the reserved spiralized vegetable soup into the puréed soup in the pan. Heat until steaming hot, then ladle into warmed soup bowls. Serve with a sprinkling of chopped fresh parsley.

Variation
For a creamy kohlrabi and apple soup, use 1 litre/1¾ pints/4 cups of stock when making the soup, then add 250ml/8fl oz/1 cup milk (semi-skimmed/low-fat or full cream/whole dairy milk or non-dairy milk such as soya or almond milk) and reheat until piping hot, but do not boil.

VT **GF** **DF** **V** **P**

Serves 4
1 large onion
15ml/1 tbsp coconut oil
1 clove garlic, peeled and crushed
5ml/1 tsp ground ginger
1.2 litres/2 pints/5 cups vegetable stock
4–5 kohlrabi, about 900g/2lb total weight, peeled
1 eating apple, peeled
Salt and ground black pepper
30ml/2 tbsp chopped fresh parsley

Based on borsch, a classic of both Russia and Poland, this stunning soup contains lots of spiralized root vegetables which all soak up the glorious red colour of the beetroot. It's essential to use good quality stock, usually beef, or canned consommé for the well-flavoured clear base. It's traditionally served with thinly sliced rye bread.

Spiralized beetroot broth

1 Spiralize the beetroot, carrot, celeriac and onion using the thin (2mm/¹⁄₁₂in) noodle blade, then snip into shorter lengths, about 4cm/1½in.

2 Heat the oil in a large pan and cook the onion over a low heat for 5 minutes, stirring occasionally. Add the garlic to the pan and cook, stirring for 1 more minute. Add the beetroot, carrot and celeriac to the pan.

3 Place the bay leaf, parsley, whole clove and peppercorns in a piece of muslin or cheesecloth and tie with string. Add to the pan with the tomatoes, then pour over the stock or consommé and stock mixture.

4 Slowly bring to the boil, reduce the heat, cover and simmer for 20–25 minutes or until the vegetables are very tender. Stir in the vinegar and adjust the seasoning if needed. Simmer for a further 2–3 minutes.

5 Meanwhile, stir the chopped dill into the sour cream and season with salt and pepper. Ladle the soup into warmed bowls and serve with the sour cream and dill in a separate bowl.

Cook's tip
To peel the tomatoes, place them in a heatproof bowl and pour over enough boiling water to cover. Leave for 30–45 seconds, then remove the tomatoes and briefly rinse under cold running water to cool. The skins should slip off easily.

GF **DF** (if sour cream not added)

Serves 4
450g/1lb uncooked beetroot (beet), peeled
1 large carrot, peeled
1 celeriac, about 400g/14oz, peeled
1 onion, peeled
15ml/1 tbsp sunflower or coconut oil
1 garlic clove, crushed
1 bay leaf
1 parsley sprig
1 whole clove
3 whole peppercorns
2 ripe tomatoes, peeled, seeded and chopped
900ml/1½ pints/3¾ cups clear beef or vegetable stock or canned beef consommé or a combination
10ml/2 tsp balsamic vinegar or the liquid from a jar of pickled beetroot (beet)
45ml/3 tbsp chopped fresh dill
150ml/¼ pint/⅔ cup sour cream (optional)
Salt and ground black pepper

For a dairy-free option, leave out the sour cream and serve the soup with a sprinkling of chopped dill

This contains the three essential ingredients of a Hungarian goulash – onions, paprika and caraway seeds – but is a lighter modern version. Low-fat breadcrumb dumplings make it a substantial lunch or supper dish, but you can leave them out of the soup if you prefer.

Paprika beef and spiralized vegetable soup

 **DF** (if using non-dairy milk)

Serves 4–6

2 onions, peeled
250g/9oz piece white cabbage
2 large carrots, peeled
30ml/2 tbsp sunflower or coconut oil
350g/12oz lean braising or chuck steak,
    trimmed and cut into 2cm/¾in cubes
2 garlic cloves, crushed
15ml/1 tbsp paprika
1.5ml/¼ tsp caraway seeds
400g/14oz can chopped tomatoes
900ml/1½ pints/3¾ cups beef stock
Salt and ground black pepper

For the dumplings:
1 courgette (zucchini), about 250g/9oz
5ml/1 tsp sunflower or coconut oil
1 egg
30ml/2 tbsp milk, dairy or plant-based
    eg soya or almond milk
115g/4oz/2 cups fresh white
    breadcrumbs

1 Spiralize the onions and white cabbage using the slicer blade and keeping the different spiralized vegetables separate, then spiralize the carrots with the medium (3mm/⅛in) noodle blade. Heat 15ml/1 tbsp oil in a large pan over a high heat. Add the beef and cook, stirring occasionally until well-browned. Remove from the pan with a slotted spoon on to a plate and set aside.

2 Heat the remaining oil in the pan, add the onions and cook over a low heat, stirring frequently for 7–8 minutes, or until softened. Add the garlic, cabbage and carrots and cook for a further minute, stirring. Sprinkle over the paprika and caraway seeds and stir, then add the tomatoes and stock. Return the beef to the pan and season with salt and pepper. Stir well, slowly bring to the boil, then cover and simmer gently for 45–50 minutes or until the beef is tender.

3 To make the dumplings, spiralize the courgette using the fine noodle (2mm/¹⁄₁₂in) blade, then cut into 2cm/¾in lengths. Heat the oil in a non-stick frying pan or skillet, add the courgette and cook over a medium heat, for about 3 minutes. Turn up the heat a little and cook for a further minute, stirring until all the juices have evaporated. Turn off the heat.

4 Beat the egg and milk together in a bowl, add the breadcrumbs and stir with a fork. Stir in the courgette and season with salt and pepper. Leave for 2–3 minutes for the breadcrumbs to soak up the liquid, then using damp hands, shape into 12 balls, each about the size of a walnut.

5 Add the dumplings to the soup, spacing slightly apart. Cover and cook over a low heat for 12–15 minutes or until the dumplings are cooked. Ladle the soup into warmed bowls, adding 3 dumplings per portion. Serve straight away.

Spiralizing courgettes and aubergines allows them to roast quickly and cook through without over-browning, giving this soup a fabulous fresh flavour. Serve with warm crusty bread such as Greek psomi and a large spoonful or two of fresh mint tzatziki.

Roasted courgette soup with minted tzatziki

1 Preheat the oven to 200°C/400°F/Gas 6. Spiralize the aubergines and courgettes using the medium noodle blade, then cut into shorter pieces about 5cm/2in long with kitchen scissors. Slice the onion using the spiralizer slicing blade. Put in a roasting pan and drizzle over the olive oil. Turn with your hands to coat the vegetables, then spread out in an even layer. Add the unpeeled garlic cloves.

2 Roast in the oven for 20–25 minutes, removing and turning the vegetables after 10 minutes, then every 5 minutes or until tender and just beginning to brown.

3 Meanwhile, make the minted tzatziki. Spiralize the cucumber using the medium noodle blade, then snip into shorter lengths about 5cm/2in long with kitchen scissors. Place in a colander, sprinkling the salt between the layers. Place over a bowl or plate and leave for 20–30 minutes.

4 Place about two-thirds of the roasted vegetables in a blender or food processor. Squeeze the roasted garlic out of its papery skin and add to the vegetables with the stock. Blend until smooth. Pour into a large pan, add the remaining roasted vegetables and season to taste with salt and pepper. Gently reheat until piping hot.

5 Squeeze the excess salty liquid out of the cucumber with your hands, then place in a bowl and stir in the yogurt and mint.

6 Ladle the soup into warmed bowls and serve topped with a spoonful or two of tzatziki and warm crusty bread. Serve the rest of the tzatziki separately.

Cook's tip
If you don't have a large blender or food processor, add just half of the stock when puréeing the vegetables; the rest of the stock can be added to the pan when reheating.

Use a well-flavoured olive oil for this soup; it will make all the difference

VT **GF** (if not served with bread)

Serves 4
2 medium aubergines (eggplants), about 600g/1lb 5oz
4 large courgettes (zucchini), about 1kg/2¼lb
1 onion, peeled
30ml/2 tbsp olive oil
2 garlic cloves, unpeeled
900ml/1½ pints/3¾ cups vegetable stock
Salt and ground black pepper

For the minted tzatziki:
1 cucumber
10ml/2 tsp salt
250ml/8fl oz/1 cup Greek (US strained plain) yogurt
30ml/2 tbsp chopped fresh mint
Crusty bread, to serve

Perfect for summer entertaining, this vegetable soup comes from the southern Spanish region of Andalusia and is always served well-chilled. A horizontal spiralizer is ideal for preparing the cucumber for this, as it will remove some of the seeded cucumber centre.

Chilled spiralizer gazpacho

Serves 4–6

2 slices day-old white bread
450ml/¾ pint/2 cups iced water
900g/2lb ripe tomatoes
1 cucumber
1 red (bell) pepper, seeded and
  roughly chopped
1 green chilli, seeded and chopped
2 cloves garlic, chopped
30ml/2 tbsp extra-virgin olive oil
Juice of 1 lime
1 small red onion, peeled
Salt and ground black pepper
Ice cubes, to serve

For the croûtons:
30ml/2 tbsp olive oil
3 thick slices bread, crusts removed and
  cut into small cubes

1 Tear the bread into small pieces and put in a blender. Pour over the water and leave to soak while preparing the other ingredients.

2 Put the tomatoes in a heatproof bowl and pour over enough boiling water to cover. Leave for 30 seconds, then drain and rinse under cold running water for a few seconds. Peel the tomatoes, quarter and remove the seeds. Add the flesh to the blender.

3 Spiralize the cucumber using the fine (2mm/¹⁄₁₂in) noodle blade. If you are using a horizontal spiralizer discard the pencil-sized core. Add half the spiralized cucumber to the blender.

4 Add the pepper, chilli, garlic, oil and lime juice to the blender with a little salt and pepper. Blend the mixture until fairly smooth, or you can leave it slightly chunky if you prefer. Cut the remaining spiralized cucumber into 4cm/1½in lengths and stir about half into the soup, reserving the rest for garnishing. If the soup is too thick, add a little more water. Cover and chill in the refrigerator for several hours or until ready to serve.

5 To make the croûtons, heat the oil in a frying pan or skillet and add the bread cubes. Cook over a medium heat, stirring occasionally to brown evenly. Drain on kitchen paper and put in a small bowl. Slice the red onion using the slicing blade on the spiralizer.

6 Ladle the gazpacho into bowls and add two or three ice cubes to each. Top with spiralized red onion and the reserved spiralized cucumber. Serve straight away and hand round the croûtons separately.

SALADS

The ultimate in healthy eating, salads can be prepared from a wide variety of spiralized vegetables and fruit with a huge range of flavours, textures and colours. They can be as simple or extravagant as you like and served as a light side or a substantial main meal. You'll find plenty of salads here which need no cooking, including raw pad Thai and sprouted salad with tofu dressing. Some vegetables benefit from brief roasting or blanching to soften and bring out all the natural sweet flavours, and these are featured in a salad of roasted spiralized beetroot and ratatouille salad. Some even have a combination of raw and cooked vegetables; spiralized Indonesian vegetable salad, more famously known as 'gado-gado' is a tantalizing taste sensation.

Raw pad Thai with spiralized noodles

Serves 4

2 large courgettes (zucchini),
about 500g/1¼lb
2 large carrots, peeled
150g/5oz piece red cabbage
1 head Chinese leaves (Chinese
cabbage), finely shredded
100g/3½oz beansprouts, rinsed

For the dressing:
2 spring onions (scallions)
1 red chilli, seeded and
finely chopped
Juice of ½ lime
75ml/5 tbsp tamari (Japanese soy sauce)
30ml/2 tbsp sesame oil
15ml/1 tbsp agave syrup

1 To make the dressing, thinly slice the spring onions on the diagonal. Place the chilli and spring onions in a bowl and squeeze over the lime juice. Add the tamari, sesame oil and agave syrup. Whisk together and leave to stand while preparing the salad; this will allow the flavours to mellow a little and permeate the dressing.

2 Spiralize the courgettes and carrots using the fine (2mm/¹⁄₁₂in) blade. Finely slice the red cabbage with the spiralizer slicing blade.

3 Place the spiralized courgettes, carrots and red cabbage in large serving bowl with the shredded Chinese leaves and beansprouts and gently mix together with your hands.

4 Whisk the dressing together again with a fork, then drizzle over the salad and gently mix together. Serve within an hour of making.

Cook's tip
Tamari is a Japanese soy sauce that is made without wheat and is therefore suitable for those on a gluten-free diet. It has a dark colour and slightly smoother, richer and less salty flavour than soy sauce.

This well-known salad is usually made with rice noodles, but courgette and carrot make a tasty alternative. Raw, plant-based foods are high in fibre and water and help you feel fuller for longer – a great lunch or side salad if you are trying to cut calories.

Roasting beetroot brings out all its naturally sweet flavours and softens the texture. Toss with toasted walnuts, orange and poppy seed dressing and watercress, which will just start to wilt in the heat.

Salad of roasted spiralized beetroot

1 Preheat the oven to 200°C/400°F/Gas 6. Spiralize the beetroot, using the medium (3mm/⅛in) noodle blade. Snip into slightly shorter lengths if you like, or leave the noodles long. Put the beetroot noodles in a roasting pan.

2 Whisk together 15ml/1 tbsp light olive oil and 15ml/1 tbsp orange juice with a little salt and ground pepper. Drizzle over the beetroot, then mix together with your hands to lightly coat. Roast in the oven for 8–12 minutes, depending on whether you prefer a firmer or softer texture.

3 Turn the spiralized beetroot, so that it will cook evenly, then push slightly to one side of the roasting pan. Add the walnut pieces, return to the oven and cook for 3–4 minutes or until the nuts are aromatic and browning very slightly; watch carefully as they can burn quickly. Remove from the oven and leave to cool for 2 minutes.

4 To make the dressing, put the mustard, orange zest and juice, olive and walnut oils and poppy seeds in a large bowl and whisk together. Add the roasted beetroot and walnuts and watercress to the dressing and gently mix together. Serve immediately, while still warm.

V   DF   GF   P   VT

Serves 4
675g/1½lb small to medium-sized
   beetroot (beet)
15ml/1 tbsp light olive oil
15ml/1 tbsp orange juice
115g/4oz/⅔ cup walnut pieces
Salt and ground black pepper
1 bunch watercress, trimmed

For the orange and poppy
seed dressing:
5ml/1 tsp Dijon mustard
2.5ml/½ tsp finely grated orange zest
15ml/1 tbsp orange juice
15ml/1 tbsp light olive oil
15ml/1 tbsp walnut oil
10ml/2 tsp poppy seeds

A cross between potato salad and coleslaw, this makes a great alternative to both and is lower in both carbohydrates and calories. The light dressing is a combination of mayonnaise and yogurt, flavoured with mustard, lemon juice and chives.

Creamy spiralized root vegetable salad

 VT **GF**

Serves 4
1 sweet potato, about 200g/7oz
1 celeriac, about 350g/12oz
1 medium turnip, about 175g/6oz

For the dressing:
5ml/1 tsp wholegrain mustard
5ml/1 tsp lemon juice or rice vinegar
30ml/2 tbsp mayonnaise
30ml/2 tbsp natural (plain) yogurt
30ml/2 tbsp snipped chives
Salt and ground black pepper

This salad works well with most types of root vegetable; try swede or beetroot for a change

1 Bring a pan of lightly salted water to the boil over a high heat. Spiralize the sweet potato, celeriac and turnip using the medium (3mm/⅛in) or preferably the thick (4mm/⅙in) noodle blade. Cut into slightly shorter, more manageable lengths.

2 When the water is boiling rapidly, add the sweet potato noodles. Heat for 2 minutes, then add the celeriac noodles, followed by the turnip noodles. Bring back to the boil and simmer for 2 minutes. The sweet potato noodles should be just cooked through and the other noodles tender, but still slightly crisp. Tip the vegetables into a colander and leave to cool for 5 minutes.

3 Meanwhile, blend the mustard with the lemon juice or rice vinegar, then stir in the mayonnaise, yogurt and chives. Season to taste with salt and pepper. Add the vegetables and gently toss together to coat in the dressing. Leave to cool completely. Serve at room temperature or chilled, if preferred.

Cook's tips
Take care not to overcook the vegetables and drain thoroughly, or the salad will be soggy. When cooling vegetables in the colander, stir occasionally to let the steam escape.

Other flavourings can be added to the dressing to complement the food accompanying the salad. Creamed horseradish works well with smoked mackerel or cold cooked beef and dill can be used instead of chives if serving with smoked salmon.

Also known as daikon and white radish, mooli is widely available in larger supermarkets and Asian stores. It can be finely spiralized into long white noodles. Here it is served in a simple dressing; don't be tempted to increase the amount of wasabi paste as it is very hot and pungent.

Spiralized mooli salad with wasabi dressing

Serves 4
2 large mooli (daikon),
    about 600g/1lb 6oz
30ml/2 tbsp rice vinegar
10ml/2 tsp wasabi paste
30ml/2 tbsp sesame oil
30ml/2 tbsp finely chopped fresh
    coriander (cilantro)
Salt and white pepper

1 Spiralize the mooli using the very fine (1mm/¹⁄₃₂in) or fine (2mm/¹⁄₁₂in) noodle blade. Blot with kitchen paper to soak up the excess juices, then place the noodles in a serving bowl. Sprinkle over 20ml/4 tsp of the vinegar and a little salt and pepper. Gently toss to coat all the noodles.

2 Blend the wasabi paste and remaining 10ml/2 tsp vinegar together. Whisk in the sesame oil, then stir in the coriander. Drizzle the dressing over the mooli and serve at room temperature.

This tempting salad has a lovely crunchy texture and makes a great accompaniment for cold fish such as smoked mackerel or poached salmon

Fennel carpaccio

1 Trim the root end and top of the fennel bulbs (save some of the feathery tops for garnishing), then finely slice using the spiralizer slicing blade. Immediately toss the slices in the orange juice to prevent them turning brown.

2 Whisk together the vinegar and oils and drizzle over the fennel, then use your hands to gently toss the slices and combine. Leave to stand at room temperature for about 30 minutes; this will allow the fennel to soften slightly.

3 Scatter the shaved Parmesan over the fennel. Sprinkle with a few chopped green feathery fronds from the fennel and grind over a little black pepper before serving.

VT **GF** **P**

Serves 4
2 large bulbs fennel, about 500g/1¼lb
Juice of 1 orange
15ml/1 tbsp white wine vinegar
15ml/1 tbsp walnut oil
30ml/2 tbsp olive oil
25g/1oz shaved Parmesan cheese, vegetarian if preferred
Ground black pepper

Raw fennel has a crunchy texture and fresh aniseed-like flavour and goes surprisingly well with tangy Parmesan. An orange dressing adds a hint of sweetness and brings the flavours together. 'Carpaccio' refers to raw food cut in paper-thin slices; sometimes meat or fish, but also raw vegetables which the spiralizer slicing blade does perfectly.

Here a combination of fresh and crunchy sprouted beans and seeds is mixed with spiralized sweet and juicy carrot and apple and served in a smooth creamy tofu dressing, which adds extra protein to the salad. It's perfect for a light lunch or supper dish.

Sprouted salad with tofu dressing

1 Spiralize the carrots and the apple. Cut into slightly shorter lengths using clean kitchen scissors. Put in a bowl, add the bean and alfalfa or sunflower seed sprouts and mix together.

2 To make the dressing, put the tofu, milk, mustard, lemon juice or rice vinegar and salt and pepper in a small food processor or blender. Blend until smooth. The dressing should be thick, but still a pourable consistency, so stir in a further 15ml/1 tbsp almond or soya milk if necessary.

3 Drizzle half the dressing over the salad and mix together to lightly coat. Drizzle the rest of the dressing over the salad, then sprinkle with toasted sesame seeds. Serve straight away.

Make sure you use silken tofu which is unpressed and has a soft creamy texture when making the dressing for this nutritious salad

V DF GF VT

Serves 4
2 medium carrots, peeled
1 green-skinned eating apple
115g/4oz mung beansprouts
50g/2oz sprouted alfalfa seeds or
  sunflower seeds
15ml/1 tbsp toasted sesame seeds

For the tofu dressing:
115g/4oz firm silken tofu
45ml/3 tbsp almond or soya milk
1.5ml/¼ tsp Dijon mustard
5ml/1 tsp lemon juice or rice vinegar
Salt and ground black pepper

Home-grown sprouts
Bean and seed sprouts are an excellent source of vitamins B and C and are easy to sprout yourself:

1 Rinse a handful or two of dried beans (not canned) or seeds, then place in a large jar. Half-fill the jar with water and cover with a piece of muslin or cheesecloth, secured firmly with elastic bands.

2 Leave to soak overnight. The following day, drain off the water through the muslin and place the jar on its side, gently shaking the beans into an even layer. Leave on a windowsill, but out of direct sunlight.

3 Fill the jar with water to rinse the beans and drain twice a day. After two or three days, sprouts will appear.

4 When the shoots are about 1cm/½in long, place in a sunny, but not too hot place. Continue to rinse and drain as before.

5 In another day or two, the shoots should be the desired length. Use before the leaves start to form, discarding any which haven't germinated. Once ready, they can be kept in a plastic bag in the refrigerator for up to 2 days.

This Indonesian main-meal salad is known as 'gado gado' meaning a mixture, and is always made of a combination of both raw and cooked vegetables; the choice depending on the season and availability. It usually has a garnish of hard-boiled eggs, although vegans can use tofu instead, and a mildly spiced creamy coconut and peanut sauce.

Spiralized Indonesian vegetable salad

VT **DF**

Serves 4
8 small new potatoes, scrubbed
4 small or medium eggs,
    at room temperature
175g/6oz fine green beans, topped
    and tailed and halved
3 medium carrots
½ cucumber
½ small head of Chinese leaves
    (Chinese cabbage), about 225g/8oz,
    finely shredded
Zested rind and juice of 1 lime
15ml/1 tbsp groundnut (peanut) or
    sunflower oil
15ml/1 tbsp soy sauce (reduced-salt,
    if you prefer)

For the spicy peanut dressing:
1 small onion, very finely chopped
1 red chilli, seeded and finely chopped
45ml/3 tbsp smooth peanut butter
5ml/1 tsp soft light brown sugar
120ml/4fl oz/½ cup canned coconut milk

1 Bring a pan of lightly salted water to the boil. Add the potatoes and cook for 14–15 minutes or until just tender. Remove from the pan with a slotted spoon and set aside to cool. Turn off the heat.

2 Lower the eggs one at a time on a spoon into the pan of near-boiling water. Bring back to the boil and simmer for 7–8 minutes. Remove from the pan and place in a bowl of cold water. Add the green beans to the boiling water and simmer for 3 minutes or until tender. Drain in a sieve or strainer and rinse under cold running water.

3 Meanwhile, put all the ingredients for the spicy peanut dressing in a small pan. Bring to the boil, then cook gently for 5 minutes, stirring occasionally. Leave until barely warm.

4 Spiralize the carrots and cucumber using the thin (2mm/1⁄12in) noodle blade. Cut into slightly shorter, more manageable lengths and pat the cucumber with kitchen paper to remove some of the moisture. Put the spiralized vegetables in a bowl with the Chinese leaves and the green beans.

5 Cut each potato into 4 pieces and add to the bowl. Whisk together the lime rind and juice, oil and soy sauce and pour over the vegetables. Mix together with your hands to lightly coat in the dressing. Transfer the vegetables to a serving platter. Shell the eggs and cut them into quarters lengthways. Arrange on top of the salad.

6 Check the consistency of the spicy peanut dressing and if it is too thick, stir in 15–30ml/1–2 tbsp water. Drizzle the dressing over the salad and serve at room temperature.

The flavours and fragrance of this salad are reminiscent of the Mediterranean and include protein-packed quinoa, toasted pine nuts, sun-dried tomatoes, basil and garlic, together with cucumber and fresh mozzarella cheese. Although mooli isn't grown in the region, it adds a crisp texture and mild peppery taste which works well here.

Quinoa salad with spiralized cucumber and mooli

 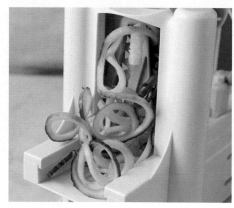 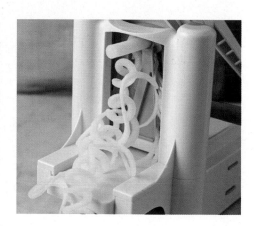

1 Dry-fry the pine nuts in a non-stick frying pan over a medium heat, for 3–4 minutes, stirring frequently, until lightly browned, taking care as they can scorch easily. Leave to cool.

2 Bring 250ml/8fl oz/1 cup water to the boil in a pan with a pinch of salt. Rinse the quinoa in a sieve or strainer under cold running water, add to the pan and cook for 15–16 minutes or until just tender. Drain off any excess water and leave to cool.

3 Put the vinegar, oil, mustard, garlic and salt and pepper to taste in a bowl and whisk together, or shake in a jar. Tear or shred the basil leaves into small pieces. Add to the dressing with the sun-dried tomatoes and stir to mix.

4 Spiralize the cucumber and mooli using the medium (3mm/⅛in) noodle blade. Cut into slightly shorter lengths and pat with kitchen paper to remove some of the juices. Place in a serving bowl and pour over the dressing. Stir to coat.

5 Add the cooled quinoa, about two-thirds of the toasted pine nuts and the mozzarella to the vegetable noodles. Mix together and serve straight away, scattering the remaining pine nuts over the top.

Cook's tip
Re-hydrate sun-dried tomatoes by placing in a heatproof bowl and generously covering with boiling water. Leave to soak for at least 1 hour and preferably 2 hours, before using. Drain well before use.

VT **GF**

Serves 4
45ml/3 tbsp pine nuts
75g/3oz/½ cup pearl quinoa
60ml/4 tbsp balsamic vinegar
30ml/2 tbsp olive oil
2.5ml/½ tsp Dijon mustard
1 garlic clove, crushed
Salt and ground black pepper
25g/1oz fresh basil leaves
50g/2oz sun-dried tomatoes, rehydrated and chopped
1 cucumber
1 mooli (daikon), about 300g/11oz
250g/9oz fresh mozzarella cheese, chopped into small pieces

Chayote and avocado salad with green chilli

Serves 4
2 firm ripe chayotes
2 firm ripe avocados

For the dressing:
45ml/3 tbsp sunflower oil
Juice of 1 lime
30ml/2 tbsp chopped fresh coriander
   (cilantro)
1 green chilli, seeded and finely chopped
Salt and ground black pepper

1 Bring a large pan of lightly salted water to the boil. Spiralize the chayotes, leaving on the skins, using the medium (3mm/⅛in) noodle blade and cut into slightly shorter manageable lengths.

2 Add the noodles to the boiling water and simmer for 3–4 minutes, until they are tender but still retain their crisp texture. Drain in a colander, then briefly rinse under cold running water and drain again. Pat dry with kitchen paper.

3 For the dressing, whisk together the oil with 15ml/1 tbsp of the lime juice. Stir in the chopped coriander and chilli, and season to taste with salt and pepper.

4 Halve the avocados and remove the stones or pits. Peel, then cut into thin slices. Toss in the remaining lime juice to prevent browning.

5 Tip the chayote noodles into a serving bowl and add the avocado. Drizzle over the dressing and gently mix together, taking care not to break up the avocado. Serve straight away.

Cook's tip
Both the chayote and dressing can be prepared ahead, but mix them together just before serving or juices may seep from the chayote and dilute the dressing.

Spiralized chayote looks very similar to courgette noodles, but the texture is denser and slightly crisper. They are delicious served with creamy avocado slices and a slightly spicy fresh lime dressing, flecked with fresh coriander and green chilli.

Vegetables retain more of their shape and texture when cooked in the oven rather than on the hob. Here, spiralized courgettes and aubergines are roasted with red onions, peppers, tomatoes and garlic until slightly caramelized and tender.

Ratatouille salad

1 Preheat the oven to 220°C/425°F/Gas 7. Spiralize the courgettes and aubergines using the medium (3mm/⅛in) noodle blade or preferably a wide (4mm/⅙in) noodle blade if your spiralizer has one. Cut into shorter lengths, about 7.5cm/3in. Slice the onion with the spiralizer slicing blade.

2 Put the courgettes, aubergines, onion, pepper and tomatoes in a large non-stick roasting pan and drizzle over 30ml/2 tbsp of the oil. Season with salt and pepper. Use your hands to turn over the vegetables and coat in the oil. Place the garlic cloves to one side of the pan.

3 Cook for 20–25 minutes, until the vegetables are tender and the edges tinged golden brown. Turn them once or twice during cooking, so they cook evenly; they should be slightly caramelized and tender. Remove from the oven and transfer to a serving dish, tipping over any juices in the pan.

4 Remove the garlic cloves and squeeze the roasted garlic into a small bowl. Mash to a paste with the remaining 30ml/2 tbsp olive oil, then whisk in the red wine vinegar. Pour the dressing over the vegetables and gently toss together. Serve at room temperature with bread and garnished with basil leaves.

    (if serving with gluten-free bread)

Serves 6
2 large courgettes (zucchini), about 450g/1lb
2 firm medium aubergines (eggplants), about 600g/1lb 5oz
1 red onion, peeled
1 yellow (bell) pepper, seeded and cut into 2cm/¾in chunks
2 large beefsteak tomatoes, cut into 2cm/¾in chunks
60ml/4 tbsp olive oil
3 garlic cloves, unpeeled
15ml/1 tbsp red wine vinegar
Salt and ground black pepper
Rustic-style bread, focaccia or gluten-free bread, to serve
Fresh basil leaves, to garnish

MEAT & POULTRY MAINS

Whatever meat you choose and whether you are looking for a simple supper or more elaborate impressive dinner-party dish, you will find plenty of recipes here for delicious pan-fried meat and poultry, stir-fries, braises and roasts. The recipes are packed with protein, vitamins and minerals and offer many ways of using spiralized vegetables and fruit. You'll find braised beef and spiralized beetroot left to slowly oven-cook and tenderize, and fantastically fast meals such as sweet seared pork with spiced red cabbage and flash-fry lamb pittas. Old favourites have been updated and include a light version of carbonara with all the flavour but a fraction of the calories, and lemon chicken, a healthy dish with all the taste of a sweet and sour.

Grating vegetables by hand when making rosti can be both time-consuming and tedious, but a spiralizer will do the hard work for you in a fraction of the time. In this dish, one large oven-baked mixed vegetable rosti is made and cut into wedges, reducing the amount of oil needed. It is the perfect accompaniment to creamy beef and mushrooms.

Beef and mushrooms with spiralized rosti

Serves 4
2 medium-sized potatoes,
    about 350g/12oz
2 medium-sized sweet potatoes,
    about 350g/12oz
1 small swede (rutabaga),
    about 350g/12oz
1 small celeriac, about 350g/12oz
Salt and ground black pepper
40g/1½oz/3 tbsp unsalted butter or
    margarine or 45ml/3 tbsp coconut or
    sunflower oil

For the beef and mushrooms:
1 large onion, peeled
450g/1lb rump steak, trimmed
30ml/2 tbsp coconut or sunflower oil
225g/8oz wild or chestnut mushrooms,
    sliced
30ml/2 tbsp well-flavoured
    vegetable stock
150ml/¼ pint/⅔ cup crème fraîche or
    Greek (US strained plain) yogurt
10ml/2 tsp wholegrain mustard
45ml/3 tbsp chopped fresh parsley

1 Preheat the oven to 200°C/400°F/Gas 6. Peel and spiralize the potatoes, sweet potatoes, swede and celeriac using the medium (3mm/⅛in) noodle blade on the spiralizer. Cut the noodles into slightly shorter lengths and use your hands to squeeze out as much excess juice as possible. Place in a large bowl, season with salt and pepper and mix together.

2 Put half the butter, margarine or oil in a large ovenproof frying pan, skillet or a 25cm/10in round baking dish. Heat in the oven for 4 minutes or until very hot, then remove and add the vegetables. Press them down to make a firm, even rosti. Dot the top with the remaining butter or margarine or drizzle with oil, then cover with foil. Bake for 20 minutes. Remove the foil and bake for a further 20 minutes or until the top is lightly browned and the vegetables cooked through.

3 While the rosti is cooking, thinly slice the onion using the slicing blade on the spiralizer. Cut the steak into thin strips, about 5cm/2in long and 5mm/¼in thick. Heat 15ml/1 tbsp oil in a non-stick frying pan, add the onion and gently cook for 10 minutes or until softened and starting to turn golden. Remove from the pan and set aside.

4 Add the rest of the oil to the pan, turn up the heat and add the beef. Stir-fry for 2–3 minutes until well-browned, but still pink in the centre. Remove from the pan with a slotted spoon and add to the onions.

5 Add the mushrooms to the pan and cook for 1–2 minutes, then lower the heat, add the vegetable stock and cook for 3–4 minutes or until tender. Stir in the crème fraîche, mustard and parsley and season with salt and pepper. Return the onions and beef to the pan and heat through, stirring, until steaming hot.

6 Turn out the rosti and cut into four triangular wedges. Place on warmed serving plates and spoon the beef and mushroom mixture over the top.

*A green vegetable such as steamed
spiralized green cabbage would make
a great accompaniment*

Here, beef is gently braised with spiralized beetroot and mild red onions, to create a rich glossy gravy. The casserole contains both capers and anchovy fillets, but their flavour isn't detectable in the finished dish; they add a wonderful savoury richness which contrasts well with the sweet earthy taste of beetroot. Serve with new potatoes and a green vegetable.

Slow-braised beef and spiralized beetroot

1 Spiralize the red onions, then the beetroot using the medium (3mm/⅛in) spiralizer blade. Snip into slightly shorter lengths using clean kitchen scissors.

2 Pat the beef dry on kitchen paper (or the beef will steam rather than brown). Heat the oil in a non-stick frying pan, then brown the meat well over a medium-high heat. Remove from the pan and set aside.

3 Add the onions to the pan and cook over medium-high heat for 2–3 minutes or until beginning to colour. Tip into a deep flameproof casserole dish and arrange the beef steaks on top.

4 Add the anchovy fillets, capers, mustard and about half of the stock to the frying pan and season with ground black pepper. Heat gently, stirring until the mustard has blended into the stock. Turn off the heat and pour over the beef. Top with the spiralized beetroot, then drizzle over the remaining stock.

5 Crumple a wet sheet of baking parchment and press down on top of the beetroot (this will help keep all the moisture and juices in the casserole). Cover the dish with a lid, place in a cold oven and heat to 160°C/325°F/Gas 3. Cook for 1½ hours.

6 Remove the lid and baking parchment and stir the ingredients together. There should be sufficient juices from the onions and beetroot, but if it is a little dry, add a few more spoonfuls of stock. Stir in the parsley, re-cover with the paper and lid and cook for a further 30 minutes or until the beef is very tender.

Serves 4
2 medium red onions, peeled
2 medium beetroot (beet), about 300g/11oz, peeled
675g/1½lb sliced braising steak, trimmed and cut into smaller steaks
30ml/2 tbsp olive or coconut oil
25g/1oz can anchovy fillets in oil, drained and roughly chopped
30ml/2 tbsp capers in vinegar, drained
5ml/1 tsp English (hot) mustard
120ml/4fl oz/½ cup beef stock
Ground black pepper
30ml/2 tbsp chopped fresh parsley

Cook's tip
Don't add salt to this dish as the anchovies are already salty. Taste and add extra seasoning to the finished dish, if needed.

This updated version of classic lasagne has a spiralized courgette noodle topping instead of traditional pasta and a lower-fat bolognese sauce thickened with red lentils. It still has the usual bubbling brown cheese sauce topping, but features a simple all-in-one sauce, rather than the more laborious and time-consuming béchamel.

Beef and courgetti lasagne

Serves 4–6
25g/1oz/3 tbsp red lentils
175ml/6fl oz/¾ cup beef stock
1 large onion, peeled
15ml/1 tbsp olive oil
115g/4oz button (white) mushrooms, sliced
1 garlic clove, crushed
400g/14oz lean minced (ground) beef steak
400g/14oz can chopped tomatoes
15ml/1 tbsp tomato purée (paste)
5ml/1 tsp dried mixed herbs
4 large courgettes (zucchini), about 1kg/2½lb

For the cheese sauce topping:
15g/½oz/2 tbsp cornflour (cornstarch)
250ml/8fl oz/1 cup milk
1 bay leaf
Salt and ground black pepper
Freshly grated nutmeg
45ml/3 tbsp freshly grated Parmesan cheese

1 Rinse the lentils in a sieve or strainer under cold running water. Tip into a bowl, pour over the stock and leave to soak for about 10 minutes. Slice the onion using the slicing blade on the spiralizer. Heat the oil in a large non-stick frying pan or skillet and gently cook the onion for 8 minutes until softened. Add the mushrooms and garlic to the pan, turn up the heat a little and cook for a further 2 minutes, stirring frequently until the onion starts to brown. Tip into the bowl with the lentils.

2 Add the beef to the pan and cook, stirring, over a high heat until browned. Stir in the tomatoes, tomato purée and herbs. Add the lentil and onion mixture and bring to the boil. Lower the heat, cover with a lid and simmer for 30 minutes or until the lentils are tender.

3 While the sauce is cooking, spiralize the courgettes using the medium (3mm/⅛in) noodle blade. Either steam the noodles for 3 minutes or boil for 1½ minutes. Tip into a colander and leave to drain over the sink for a few minutes, stirring occasionally to release the steam.

4 For the cheese sauce topping, blend the cornflour with 45ml/3 tbsp of the milk in a pan. Heat the remaining milk and bay leaf in a jug or pitcher in the microwave until steaming hot, then whisk the hot milk into the cornflour mixture. Bring to the boil, stirring all the time and simmer for 1 minute. Remove and discard the bay leaf, then season with salt, pepper and freshly grated nutmeg to taste.

5 Preheat the oven to 180°C/350°F/Gas 4. Spoon the meat sauce into a 2.4 litre/4 pint/10 cup ovenproof dish, then spread the courgette noodles on top. Pour over the white sauce, spreading into an even layer. Sprinkle the Parmesan cheese over the top and place the dish on a baking sheet. Bake for 30 minutes or until well-browned and bubbling.

Cook's tips
The meat sauce should be very thick, as juices from the courgettes (zucchini) will dilute it as it cooks.

You can also use this sauce as bolognese to serve on top of plates of steamed or boiled courgette noodles. Cook it on the hob for an extra 15–20 minutes.

Stir-frying is a great way to combine a small amount of meat with spiralized vegetables to make a quick meal in one pan. This is a Japanese-style version and includes cucumber, which is surprisingly good stir-fried. Prepare it on a horizontal spiralizer if you have one, to remove some of the seeds from the centre.

Teryaki beef spiralized stir-fry

1 Trim the beef if necessary and cut into 1cm/½in wide strips. Whisk together the tamari, mirin or sherry, garlic, ginger and sugar in a bowl. Add the beef and stir to coat. Leave to marinate at room temperature for at least 30 minutes, or preferably for several hours, or overnight in the refrigerator.

2 Spiralize the courgettes using the medium (3mm/⅛in) noodle blade. Spiralize the carrots and cucumber with the thin (2mm/¹⁄₁₂in) blade, then cut into slightly shorter lengths.

3 Bring a pan of lightly salted water to the boil. Add the courgette noodles and bring back to the boil. Simmer for 2–3 minutes or until tender. Tip into a colander and drain well.

4 Meanwhile, heat 15ml/1 tbsp of oil in a wok or large non-stick frying pan or skillet until very hot. Remove the beef from the marinade and add to the pan and cook for about 45 seconds, stirring constantly until browned all over but still tender in the middle. Remove from the pan with a slotted spoon and set aside.

5 Add the remaining 15ml/1 tbsp oil to the pan and cook the carrots, cucumber and spring onions over a high heat for 2–3 minutes, stirring frequently until tender. Return the beef to the pan with any remaining marinade and stir-fry until the beef is hot and cooked to your liking.

6 Divide the courgette noodles between warmed bowls or serving plates. Top with the beef, carrot and cucumber stir-fry and serve straight away, garnished with a few pieces of pickled sushi ginger.

Serves 4
350g/12oz beef fillet
60ml/4 tbsp tamari (Japanese soy sauce)
60ml/4 tbsp mirin or medium sherry
1 garlic clove, peeled and finely chopped
2.5cm/1in piece fresh root ginger, peeled and grated
2.5ml/½ tsp soft light brown sugar
2 large courgettes (zucchini), about 500g/1¼lb
2 large carrots, peeled
1 cucumber
30ml/2 tbsp groundnut (peanut) or sunflower oil
6 spring onions (scallions), trimmed and sliced on the diagonal
Few pieces of pickled sushi ginger, cut into fine strips, to garnish

Marinating the beef will add flavour and tenderize at the same time

Venison is an excellent source of protein, potassium, phosphorus and B vitamins. It has the lowest fat content of any red meat and twice as much iron as beef. Its rich flavour is complemented with an apple juice marinade, which works well with roasted beetroot and sweet potatoes. Serve with a green vegetable for a satisfying and healthy meal.

Venison medallions on a bed of spiralized beetroot and sweet potato

1 Trim the medallions if necessary and place in a shallow dish. Whisk together the apple juice, lemon juice, 15ml/1 tbsp of the olive oil and juniper berries in a small bowl and pour over the medallions, turning them to coat all over. Cover and marinate in the refrigerator for at least 2 hours, preferably overnight.

2 For the spiralized vegetables, spiralize the onion using the medium (3mm/ ⅛in) noodle blade. Put the noodles in a heatproof bowl and pour over plenty of boiling water to cover (this will soften the onion before roasting and start the cooking process).

3 Put a large non-stick roasting pan in the oven and preheat the oven to 200°C/ 400°F/Gas 6. Spiralize the beetroot and sweet potato using the medium (3mm/ ⅛in) noodle blade. Drain the sliced onion in a colander, then tip back into the bowl. Add the spiralized beetroot and sweet potatoes, drizzle over the 15ml/ 1 tbsp olive oil and season with salt and pepper. Mix together to lightly coat all the vegetables with oil (wear clean rubber gloves if you like, to stop the beetroot staining your hands). Tip the vegetables into the hot roasting pan. Roast for 15 minutes or until the vegetables are tender and beginning to char in places, turning halfway through cooking time, so that they cook evenly.

4 Meanwhile, heat the remaining 15ml/1 tbsp of the olive oil in a non-stick frying pan, skillet or a ridged griddle pan over a high heat. Remove the medallions from the marinade and pat dry on kitchen paper. Add to the pan and cook for 3–5 minutes, depending on how done you like the meat, then turn over and cook for a further 2–3 minutes; the outside should be dark and slightly charred and the middle still very or slightly pink. Transfer to a warm plate, cover with foil and leave to rest for 2–3 minutes.

5 Pour the stock into the pan and allow it to bubble for a minute. Add the port and simmer for a further 2 minutes so that the alcohol evaporates. Stir in the horseradish sauce.

6 Arrange the noodles on four warmed serving plates and top each with a venison medallion. Drizzle the sauce over the top and serve straight away with green beans or tenderstem broccoli.

DF **GF**

Serves 4
4 medallions of loin of venison, about
   4cm/1½in thick
60ml/4 tbsp apple juice
15ml/1 tbsp lemon juice
30ml/2 tbsp olive oil
5ml/1 tsp crushed juniper berries
75ml/2½fl oz/⅓ cup beef stock
30ml/2 tbsp port
5ml/1 tsp hot horseradish sauce
Green beans or tenderstem broccoli,
   to serve

For the spiralized vegetables:
1 large red onion, peeled
450g/1lb medium-sized beetroot (beet)
1 large sweet potato, about 250g/9oz
15ml/1 tbsp olive oil
Salt and ground black pepper

These deliciously healthy burgers are made with lean minced pork, a spiralized tart cooking apple and cooked quinoa, a protein-rich supergrain. Flavoured with Chinese five-spice powder, a warm pungent mix that includes star anise and cinnamon, they make a great sizzling summer barbecue or quick supper dish, served with tender pak choi.

Five-spice pork and spiralized apple patties

Serves 4

40g/1½oz/¼ cup quinoa (white, red, black or mixed)
125ml/4fl oz/½ cup light vegetable stock or water
1 medium onion, peeled
1 medium cooking apple
45ml/3 tbsp vegetable oil
2 cloves garlic, crushed
450g/1lb minced (ground) lean pork
10ml/2 tsp Chinese five-spice powder
5ml/1 tsp wholegrain mustard
1 egg, beaten
50g/2oz/½ cup quinoa flour
Salt and ground black pepper
Steamed pak choi (bok choy) and soy sauce or tamari (Japanese soy sauce), to serve

1 Rinse the quinoa in water. Put in a pan with the stock or water, bring to the boil, cover and simmer for 14–16 minutes until all of the water is absorbed. Tip into a large bowl.

2 Slice the onion using the spiralizer slicing blade. Peel and spiralize the cooking apple using the fine (2mm/¹⁄₁₂in) noodle blade. Cut the spiralized apple into shorter lengths with kitchen scissors.

3 Heat 15ml/1 tbsp of the oil in a non-stick frying pan or skillet. Add the onion and cook for 3 minutes, then add the apple and garlic and fry for a further 4–5 minutes, until softened. Add to the bowl containing the cooked quinoa. Leave to cool for a few minutes.

4 Add the pork, five-spice powder and mustard to the bowl, together with the beaten egg, flour and seasoning. Use your hands to mix the ingredients together until well combined.

5 With slightly dampened hands, to help prevent sticking, shape the mixture into 8 burger-size 'patties' and set them aside on a floured board.

6 Wash and dry the frying pan, heat the remaining 30ml/2 tbsp oil in the pan and fry the patties on high heat for 3–4 minutes. Flip the patties and fry on the other side for another 3 minutes, then reduce the heat and cook for a further 6–8 minutes, until cooked through and no longer pink in the middle. Serve with steamed pak choi and a dash of soy sauce or tamari.

Marinating pieces of pork flavours the meat and tenderizes it at the same time. Serving with spiralized red cabbage stir-fried with red wine, balsamic vinegar and warm spices complements and contrasts with the richness of the meat, and tastes delicious too.

Sweet seared pork with spiralized red cabbage

1 Remove the rind and layer of fat from the pork, then cut the meat into small even-sized pieces. Mix the soy sauce, Worcestershire sauce, honey, mustard, vinegar, tomato purée and herbs together in a bowl. Add the meat and stir until all the pieces are coated. Cover and leave to marinate at room temperature for 30 minutes, or preferably for several hours or overnight in the refrigerator.

2 Spiralize the red onions and cabbage with the spiralizer slicing blade. Heat 15ml/1 tbsp of the oil in a wok or large non-stick frying pan, add the onions and cook over a medium heat for 4–5 minutes, stirring frequently until softened. Add the red cabbage, 100ml/3½fl oz/scant ½ cup of the wine, stock, vinegar, star anise, garlic and sugar. Cook, stirring for a few seconds, then cover the pan, lower the heat and simmer gently for 5 minutes or until the vegetables are just tender. Turn off the heat.

3 Meanwhile, heat the remaining 15ml/1 tbsp oil in a non-stick frying pan, add the pork and stir-fry over a high heat for 5 minutes or until well-browned. Lower the heat and cook for a further 2–3 minutes, until cooked through and tender. Add the remaining 50ml/2fl oz/¼ cup of red wine to the pan and let it bubble for a minute, stirring.

4 Remove the lid from the cabbage and reheat for a minute or two, allowing most of the excess liquid to evaporate. Divide between warmed plates and serve topped with the pork mixture.

Serves 4
675g/1½lb pork belly
15ml/1 tbsp soy sauce
15ml/1 tbsp Worcestershire sauce
15ml/1 tbsp honey
15ml/1 tbsp wholegrain mustard
10ml/2 tsp balsamic vinegar
10ml/2 tsp tomato purée (paste)
5ml/1 tsp dried mixed herbs

For the spiced red cabbage:
2 red onions, peeled
Small red cabbage, about 450g/1lb
30ml/2 tbsp sunflower or coconut oil
150ml/¼ pint/⅔ cup red wine
75ml/5 tbsp vegetable or light
  chicken stock
15ml/1 tbsp balsamic vinegar
3 star anise
1 garlic clove, crushed
10ml/2 tsp light muscovado
  (brown) sugar

Red wine adds flavour and colour to both the pork and cabbage and the alcohol evaporates as it cooks

Fillet is the leanest and healthiest cut of pork, needs little preparation and takes less than half an hour to roast. Here it is given a flavoursome coating and briefly roasted until tender, then combined with a selection of fresh vegetables to add taste and texture.

Red-roasted pork with spiralized courgette and carrot noodles

Serves 4
450g/1lb pork fillet
15ml/1 tbsp dark soy sauce
15ml/1 tbsp hoisin sauce
5ml/1 tsp light muscovado (brown) sugar
5ml/1 tsp sunflower oil
2.5ml/½ tsp five-spice powder
4 drops natural red food colouring (optional)
2.5cm/1in piece fresh ginger, grated

For the noodles:
2 large carrots
2 large courgettes (zucchini), about 500g/1¼lb
10ml/2 tsp groundnut (peanut) or coconut oil
10ml/2 tsp sesame oil
2 garlic cloves, finely chopped
6 spring onions (scallions), trimmed and cut into 2cm/¾in lengths diagonally
115g/4oz chestnut mushrooms, sliced
45ml/3 tbsp yellow bean sauce
30ml/2 tbsp dry sherry
30ml/2 tbsp dark soy sauce

1 Trim off any visible fat from the pork. Put the soy sauce, hoisin sauce, sugar, oil, five-spice powder and food colouring if using, into a bowl. Squeeze the juices from the ginger into the bowl and mix everything together. Spread the mixture over the pork, cover and marinate for 2 hours, or overnight in the refrigerator, if preferred.

2 Remove the pork from the refrigerator and place on a rack over a foil-lined roasting pan. Leave at room temperature for a few minutes while preheating the oven to 200°C/400°F/Gas 6. Roast for 5 minutes, then lower the oven temperature to 180°C/350°F/Gas 4 and roast for a further 20 minutes, basting occasionally. Remove from the oven, cover with foil and leave to rest for 5 minutes, then cut into thin slices.

3 Spiralize the carrots and courgettes using the medium (3mm/⅛in) spiralizer noodle blade. Place in a steamer over boiling water and cook for 3 minutes or drop into boiling water and cook for 3 minutes until just tender (if cooking in boiling water, add the carrots first and leave for a few seconds before adding the courgettes). Tip into a colander and drain well.

4 Heat a wok or large non-stick frying pan and add the oils. Add the garlic and spring onions and stir-fry for a few seconds, then add the mushrooms and stir-fry for a further 1–2 minutes. Add the bean sauce, sherry and soy sauce, stir, then add the noodles and sliced pork. Cook over a high heat, stirring all the time for 1–2 minutes until hot. Serve straight away.

Cook's tip
Check to see if the pork is cooked by inserting a thin skewer into the middle and leaving for a few seconds. The skewer should be hot and the juices run clear.

The flavour of this dhansak-style curry is enhanced with spiralized butternut squash which soaks up the freshly ground spices and adds a subtle sweetness to the finished dish. Traditional rice makes a good accompaniment or you could serve with spiralized vegetable rice; celeriac or aubergine rice would work well here.

Spiced lamb with lentils and spiralized butternut squash

1 Trim the fat from the lamb and cut the meat into 2cm/¾in cubes. Rinse the lentils in a sieve or strainer under cold running water, then tip into a small bowl. Pour over enough water to cover by about 5cm/2in, then leave to soak.

2 Crush the cumin and cardamom seeds, peppercorns and chilli flakes in a pestle and mortar or an electric spice grinder. Spiralize the onion using the spiralizer slicing blade.

3 Heat 15ml/1 tbsp of the oil in a large pan or flameproof casserole, add the lamb and fry over a high heat for 3–4 minutes or until browned all over. Remove from the pan with a slotted spoon and set aside.

4 Heat the remaining 15ml/1 tbsp oil in the pan or casserole, add the onion and fry gently for 5 minutes, stirring frequently. Add the garlic and ginger and cook for 2–3 minutes. Add the cinnamon stick and sprinkle over the turmeric. Stir, then return the lamb to the pan and add the stock and tomatoes. Bring to the boil, reduce the heat, cover and gently simmer for 45 minutes. Drain the lentils and stir into the curry. Re-cover and simmer for a further 15 minutes.

5 Spiralize the butternut squash using the 3mm/⅛in (medium) spiralizer noodle blade. Cut into shorter lengths, about 7.5cm/3in with clean kitchen scissors. Stir into the curry, then simmer for a further 15–20 minutes or until the lamb, lentils and butternut squash are very tender. Stir in the lemon juice and fresh coriander and season to taste with salt and pepper. Serve in warm bowls.

DF **GF** **P** (if coconut oil used not sunflower oil)

Serves 4
450g/1lb lean boneless neck fillet or leg of lamb
175g/6oz/1 cup green lentils
15ml/1 tbsp cumin seeds
Seeds from 6 cardamom pods
6 black peppercorns
Pinch of dried chilli flakes
1 medium onion, peeled
30ml/2 tbsp sunflower or coconut oil
2 garlic cloves, crushed
5cm/2in piece fresh root ginger, peeled and grated
1 cinnamon stick
7.5ml/1½ tsp ground turmeric
600ml/1 pint/2½ cups lamb or vegetable stock
225g/8oz can chopped tomatoes
350g/12oz piece butternut squash, peeled
15ml/1 tbsp lemon juice
45ml/3 tbsp chopped fresh coriander (cilantro)
Salt and ground black pepper

Served in wholemeal pitta pockets with a spiralized red onion and carrot salad, quick-cooked lamb fillet makes a simple yet nutritious and filling lunch or supper. The salad is briefly marinated to soften and mellow the flavour of the onions and to add flavour as well.

Flash-fry lamb and spiralized salad pittas

Serves 4
450g/1lb lamb neck fillet
Juice of 1 large lemon
45ml/3 tbsp olive oil
1 garlic clove, crushed
7.5ml/1½ tsp finely chopped
    rosemary leaves
1 medium red onion, peeled
1 large carrot, peeled
4 wholemeal (whole-wheat) pitta breads
1 Little Gem lettuce, separated
    into leaves
Salt and ground black pepper

*Serve the pittas with
some minted tzatziki
(see page 83) to spoon into
the filled pitta pockets*

1 Cut the lamb into thick slices, then cut it into strips across the grain of the meat. Whisk the lemon juice and olive oil together in a medium bowl and season with a little salt and pepper. Drizzle half of the lemon and oil mixture over the meat and add the garlic and rosemary leaves. Mix together with your hands until all the pieces of meat are coated in the mixture. Cover and leave to marinate at room temperature for 30 minutes.

2 Spiralize the onion using the fine (2mm/¹⁄₁₂in) spiralizer noodle blade. Cut into more manageable shorter lengths, about 5cm/2in long, using clean kitchen scissors. Put in a bowl and drizzle over the remaining lemon and oil mixture. Mix well to coat the onion in the mixture. Spiralize the carrot and cut into shorter more manageable lengths and add to the onions, then mix together. Cover the bowl with a piece of clear film or plastic wrap and leave at room temperature.

3 Heat a wok or large non-stick frying pan and stir-fry half the lamb strips for 4–5 minutes, until browned and tender. Remove and set aside, then repeat with the remaining lamb (frying in smaller batches will allow the lamb to quickly brown rather than steam).

4 Sprinkle the pitta breads lightly with water on both sides and warm under a medium grill or broiler for about 2 minutes, turning halfway through (the water will stop them burning and keep them moist). Split open the pittas to make pockets.

5 Add the lettuce leaves to the onion and carrot mixture (you may not need all the leaves; the smaller ones are best for filling the pittas) and mix to coat the leaves in some of the dressing. Divide the lamb and salad mixture between the pittas and serve with minted tzatziki.

In this low-carbohydrate, cream-free carbonara, the heat from the steaming hot spiralized courgettes lightly cooks the creamy egg and cheese sauce. Make sure you have all the individual ingredients prepared before you start to cook and warmed bowls ready, as carbonara should be served as soon as the sauce has thickened.

Courgetti carbonara

1 Heat a wok or large non-stick frying pan and add the pancetta. Cook over a medium-high heat for 3–4 minutes or until golden and crisp, stirring frequently. Add the garlic and stir for a further 30 seconds. Tip out on to kitchen paper to blot up excess fat. Wipe the excess fat from the pan with kitchen paper, but leave any of the crusty bits as these will flavour the sauce.

2 Spiralize the courgettes using the medium (3mm/⅛in) spiralizer noodle blade. Bring a large pan of lightly salted water to the boil, add the courgettes and cook for 2–3 minutes or until barely tender. Tip into a colander and drain well, reserving 75ml/5 tbsp of the cooking water.

3 Beat together the whole eggs, yolks and Parmesan and season generously with pepper. Stir in the reserved cooking water (it should be warm but not boiling or it will start to cook the eggs).

4 Tip the spiralized courgettes into the wok or large frying pan and heat, for a minute or two, stirring to evaporate some of the moisture from the courgettes. Turn off the heat.

GF

Serves 4
115g/4oz pancetta, finely chopped
1 clove garlic, peeled and finely chopped
4 large courgettes (zucchini),
   about 1kg/2¼lb
2 whole eggs
4 egg yolks
50g/2oz Parmesan cheese, finely grated
Salt and ground black pepper

5 Whisk the reserved cooking water into the egg mixture, then pour over the courgettes, stirring until the sauce is thickened and creamy. Stir in the pancetta and serve immediately on warmed plates.

Cook's tip
If the heat of the courgettes doesn't cook and thicken the egg sauce enough, cook very briefly over a low heat, stirring.

This is worlds apart from the typical take-away sweet and sour of deep-fried battered chicken and vibrant-coloured gloopy sauce. Here, coated strips of lean, tender chicken are flash-fried in a tiny amount of oil and served in a tasty sauce with spiralized onion, courgette noodles and beansprouts, for deliciously healthy dining.

Lemon chicken with courgetti

 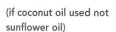 (if coconut oil used not sunflower oil)

Serves 4

4 skinless, boneless chicken breasts
Grated zest and juice of 1 lemon
45ml/3 tbsp wholegrain mustard
15ml/1 tbsp clear honey
15ml/1 tbsp sesame oil
1 onion, peeled
2 large courgettes (zucchini),
    about 500g/1¼lb
30ml/2 tbsp sunflower or coconut oil
175g/6oz beansprouts
30ml/2 tbsp sesame seeds
15ml/1 tbsp tomato purée (paste)

1 Cut the chicken breasts into thin strips. Put 30ml/2 tbsp of the lemon juice, mustard, honey and sesame oil in a bowl and whisk them together. Add the chicken strips and stir until well-coated in the mixture. Leave to stand for a few minutes while preparing the vegetables.

2 Spiralize the onion and courgettes using the medium (3mm/⅛in) spiralizer noodle blade. Cut the noodles into shorter lengths, about 10cm/4in.

3 Heat a wok or large non-stick frying pan and add 15ml/1 tbsp of the sunflower or coconut oil. Add the onion and stir-fry over a medium-low heat for 5 minutes, or until softened. Add the courgettes and stir-fry for 1 minute, then add the beansprouts and stir-fry for a further 2–3 minutes or until all the vegetables are tender. Using a slotted spoon, remove the vegetables from the pan and set aside.

4 Heat 10ml/2 tsp of the remaining oil in the wok or pan until very hot, add half the coated chicken strips and stir-fry for 6–7 minutes or until the chicken is tender and golden. Remove with a slotted spoon, leaving any oil and juices behind and set aside. Repeat with the remaining 5ml/1 tsp oil and chicken. Return the first batch of chicken to the pan. Add the sesame seeds and cook for a further minute or until the seeds start to colour.

5 Mix together the remaining lemon juice, lemon zest and tomato purée with 30ml/2 tbsp water. Return the vegetables and any juices to the pan with the lemon and tomato mixture and gently reheat, stirring until everything is coated with the sauce. Serve straight away.

This light chicken loaf is wrapped in thin slices of courgette and looks lovely when made with both green and yellow varieties; the slicing blade on a vertical spiralizer is best for cutting these. Inside, spiralized courgette noodles keep the chicken mixture beautifully moist as it cooks. It's delicious served with a crunchy fruit and vegetable salad. Serve warm or leave the loaf in the tin and turn out when almost cold.

Chicken layered loaf with spiralized salad

1 Trim the ends off the courgettes, then cut a lengthways slice to the middle of 2 of the courgettes (this will enable you to create single rather than concertina slices) and slice using the slicing blade on the spiralizer. Spiralize the remaining 2 courgettes using the medium (3mm/⅛in) spiralizer noodle blade.

2 Heat a ridged cast-iron grill or broiling pan, then brush with 5ml/1 tsp of the oil. Grill or broil the courgette slices, in batches, until the slices have charred lines and are just tender, turning once to cook both sides. Add a little more oil to the pan.

3 Cut the spiralized courgette noodles into 7.5cm/3in lengths. Heat the remaining 15ml/1 tbsp oil in a wok or large non-stick frying pan. Add the spring onions and stir-fry for 2 minutes, then add the garlic and courgette noodles. Continue to cook over a medium-low heat for 3–4 minutes, stirring frequently until just softened. Add the mustard and stir for a further minute. Tip into a colander on a plate and leave to cool (a small amount of liquid will drain on to the plate as the courgettes cool, and should be discarded).

4 Put the chicken in a bowl and add the spiralized vegetable mixture. Season well. Using your hands, mix all the ingredients together. Place a roasting pan half-filled with hot water in the oven and preheat to 180°C/350°F/Gas 4.

5 Use the grilled or broiled courgette slices to line the base and slightly up the sides of a 900g/2lb loaf tin or pan, overlapping the slices slightly. Spoon in some of the chicken and courgette mixture, pressing lightly and pushing the mixtures into the corners, then add another row of courgette slices up the sides and more chicken mixture. Repeat until all the chicken is used up, then smooth the top level and arrange the remaining courgette slices on the top.

6 Cover the top with foil and place the loaf tin in the roasting pan of water. If necessary, pour in a little more hot water to reach about two-thirds of the way up the tin. Cook for 1 hour, or until the loaf is cooked through; the juices should run clear when a skewer is inserted into the middle. Remove the loaf and leave to stand for 10 minutes, then pour off the juices before slicing.

7 To make the salad, spiralize the apple and pear using the fine (2mm/¹⁄₁₂in) spiralizer noodle blade. Place in a bowl and sprinkle over the orange juice and mix well. Spiralize the carrot using the same blade and add to the fruit (cut all the noodles into slightly shorter lengths if you prefer), then spiralize the cabbage using the spiralizer slicing blade. Whisk together the olive oil, honey and white wine vinegar and season. Pour over the fruit and vegetables and gently mix everything together.

DF **GF** **P**

Serves 4
4 large courgettes (zucchini), around 1kg/2¼lb, preferably 2 green and 2 yellow
30ml/2 tbsp olive oil
Bunch of spring onions (scallions), thinly sliced
2 garlic cloves, peeled and crushed
5ml/1 tsp Dijon mustard
500g/1¼lb minced (ground) chicken
Salt and ground black pepper

For the salad:
1 red-skinned apple
1 pear
30ml/2 tbsp orange juice
2 medium carrots
225g/8oz red or white cabbage, or a mixture of both
15ml/1 tbsp olive oil
10ml/2 tsp clear honey
5ml/1 tsp white wine vinegar

Cook's tip
If you don't have a ridged grill or broiling pan, lightly brush the courgette slices with oil and cook under a medium grill or broiler for 6–7 minutes, turning once, until tender and just beginning to brown.

This colourful dish is simple to make and contains 'rice' created from spiralized butternut squash. It includes a small amount of chicken with additional protein provided by nuts and beans. Warm ginger, cinnamon and coriander add a fragrant note to this well-balanced meal. For a vegetarian version, leave out the chicken and increase the nuts and beans.

Chicken and almond pilaf with spiralized rice

Serves 4

75g/3oz/¾ cup blanched almonds
1 large butternut squash
2 onions, peeled
30ml/2 tbsp olive oil
2 chicken breasts, cut into 2cm/¾in cubes
2 garlic cloves, peeled and crushed
4cm/1½in piece fresh root ginger, peeled and grated
1 red chilli, deseeded and sliced
10ml/2 tsp ground coriander
2.5ml/½ tsp ground turmeric
1 cinnamon stick, halved
175ml/6fl oz/¾ cup chicken or vegetable stock
150g/5oz green beans, halved
200g/7oz can beans, such as pinto or mixed beans, peas and lentils, drained and rinsed
30ml/2 tbsp chopped fresh coriander (cilantro)
Salt and ground black pepper

Cook's tip
If you want to make this a paleo dish, leave out the canned beans.

1 Put the almonds in a heatproof bowl and pour over plenty of boiling water to cover. Leave to soak and soften for at least 30 minutes or for several hours if time allows. Drain, reserving the liquid, then cut the almonds in half lengthways.

2 Brown the almonds in a small non-stick frying pan over a medium-low heat. Take care as they burn quickly; remove from the heat as soon as they start to colour as they will continue cooking in the residual heat for a while.

3 Meanwhile, spiralize the butternut squash and onions, using the fine (2mm/1⁄12in) spiralizer blade. Snip the butternut squash noodles into shorter lengths and place in a food processor. Pulse until the pieces are chopped into small lengths and resemble grains of rice in size.

4 Cut the spiralized onions into 7.5cm/3in lengths. Heat the oil in a large pan, add the onions and cook for 5–6 minutes or until almost soft. Add the chicken pieces and stir-fry for 2–3 minutes or until no longer pink. Add the garlic, ginger, chilli, ground coriander, turmeric and cinnamon and stir for a further minute.

5 Add the stock, green beans and spiralized butternut squash. Stir well, then cover and cook over a low heat for 5–7 minutes, shaking the pan occasionally until the chicken, squash and beans are just cooked through.

6 Remove the lid and stir in the canned beans. Season to taste with salt and ground black pepper. Continue to cook over a low heat for 2 minutes, stirring occasionally until piping hot. The pilaf should be fairly dry, so if the butternut squash has produced too much juice, put over a high, rather than low heat for the last 2 minutes to evaporate some of the liquid, stirring frequently. Stir in the coriander and toasted almonds before serving.

Using a spiralizer is a great way to produce fine and even potato slices. Here, they are lightly salted to draw out excess water, then arranged in overlapping circles; the starch in potatoes will ensure they stick together as they cook. The resulting galettes are then served with a tasty chicken liver topping with spiralized carrot, sage and onion.

Sautéed chicken livers with sage and onion on spiralized potato galettes

1 Make a lengthways cut to the centre of each potato, then slice using the spiralizer slicer blade (a vertical spiralizer is preferable for this, as a horizontal one will create a hole in the middle of each slice). Layer the slices in a colander on a plate or over the sink, sprinkling a little salt between the layers, then leave to drain for 10 minutes.

2 Meanwhile, spiralize the carrot and onion using the fine (2mm/¹⁄₁₂in) spiralizer noodle blade. Cut the noodles into 7.5cm/3in lengths with clean kitchen scissors.

3 Rinse the potatoes under cold running water, then pat dry with kitchen paper. Arrange the slices into 4 circles, overlapping the slices; you will need about 8 slices of potato for each. Heat 15ml/1 tbsp of the oil in the frying pan and using a fish slice, carefully transfer a galette to the pan. Cook over a moderate heat for 5–6 minutes, turning once until well-browned and cooked through. Keep warm while making the remaining galettes, adding more oil to the pan when necessary.

4 Heat 15ml/1 tbsp of the oil in a frying pan, add the onion and cook over a moderate heat for 3–4 minutes. Add the garlic and carrot and cook for a further minute. Turn off the heat and tip the vegetable mixture into a bowl. Wipe out the pan with kitchen paper.

5 Heat the remaining 15ml/1 tbsp oil in the pan, add the chicken livers, and cook, stirring to brown on all sides. As they cook, break up any large livers into bite-sized pieces. Add the stock, balsamic vinegar and sage and stir well. Return the onions and carrots to the pan and continue cooking for 7–8 minutes, or until the livers are just cooked through and the sauce very thick.

6 Transfer the potato galettes to warmed plates and divide the chicken liver mixture between them. Garnish with sprigs of fresh sage and serve with a mixed side salad.

Chicken livers make a tasty dish that is both nutritious and economical. Best of all, they need little preparation

GF **DF** **P** (if coconut oil used not sunflower oil)

Serves 4

For the potato galettes:
2 large potatoes, about 450g/1lb
10ml/2 tsp salt
30ml/2 tbsp coconut or sunflower oil

For the sage and onion chicken livers:
1 large carrot, peeled
1 red onion, peeled
2 garlic cloves, finely chopped
30ml/2 tbsp coconut or sunflower oil
400g/14oz chicken livers, trimmed
60ml/4 tbsp well-flavoured chicken or
    vegetable stock
45ml/3 tbsp balsamic vinegar
15ml/1 tbsp shredded fresh sage
Ground black pepper
Small sprigs of fresh sage, to garnish
Mixed salad, to serve

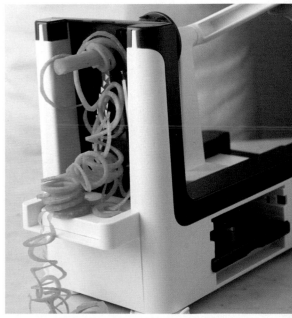

Minced turkey is much leaner than either beef or pork mince, but it can lack flavour, so here it is used together with spiralized onions and butternut squash in a chilli-tomato sauce to make a tasty filling for soft wholemeal tortillas. Topping with a little crème fraîche and a sprinkling of cheese, grilled until bubbling, adds the perfect finishing touch.

Turkey enchiladas with spiralized vegetables

Serves 4

2 medium red onions, peeled
350g/12oz piece butternut squash, peeled
15ml/1 tbsp olive oil
2 cloves garlic
2 fresh green chillies, halved, seeded and finely chopped
225g/8oz minced (ground) turkey
10ml/2 tsp each ground coriander and cumin
200g/7oz can chopped tomatoes
1 chicken or vegetable stock (bouillon) cube
7.5ml/1½ tsp chopped fresh oregano or 2.5ml/½ tsp dried
8 wholemeal (whole-wheat) flour tortillas
120ml/8 tbsp crème fraîche or sour cream
75g/3oz mature (sharp) Cheddar cheese, grated
Salt and ground black pepper

1 Slice the onions using the spiralizer slicing blade. Spiralize the butternut squash using the medium (3mm/⅛in) noodle blade. Cut into 7.5cm/3in lengths with clean kitchen scissors.

2 Heat the oil in a large pan over a medium heat. Add the onion and cook, stirring for 3–4 minutes, then crush the garlic into the pan. Stir in two-thirds of the chopped chillies, followed by the turkey, ground coriander and cumin. Stir for a few minutes, using a wooden spoon to break up the turkey, until the meat is no longer pink.

3 Stir in the tomatoes and their juice and add the stock cube. Stir until dissolved, then add the oregano and butternut squash and season with salt and pepper. Bring to the boil, then lower the heat, cover and simmer gently for 7–8 minutes, stirring occasionally, until the butternut squash is just tender. Remove the lid, turn up the heat a little and cook for a few more minutes or until the sauce is very thick.

4 Preheat the grill or broiler to high while assembling the enchiladas. Spoon some turkey mixture along the centre of each tortilla. Roll up like a pancake and place in a heatproof gratin dish. Continue until all the mixture is used up and all the tortillas are filled. If you can't fit all 8 enchiladas in the dish, use 2 smaller dishes.

5 Spoon over the crème fraîche or sour cream and scatter with the grated cheese. Place under the grill and cook until lightly browned and bubbling. Sprinkle over the remaining chopped chilli before serving.

Although duck breast is often served with the skin, this is very high in fat and calories. Here, the skin is left on during cooking to keep the breast beautifully moist and tender, then removed before slicing and serving. Roasting with just a little oil and fruit juice brings out all the flavour of the fresh vegetables and keeps them moist during cooking.

Aromatic duck with spiralized potato and beetroot ribbons

1 Ease the skin from the duck breasts but don't detach it completely. Squeeze the juice from the ginger into a bowl. Add the sesame oil, cinnamon, soy sauce, rice wine or sherry and sugar. Stir together, then add the duck breasts to the bowl and use your hands to coat the meat all over, including under the skin. Cover and leave to marinate at room temperature for 20 minutes, or for several hours in the refrigerator.

2 Cut the onions into wedges, keeping them intact at the root ends. Cut the sugar snap peas or mangetouts in half lengthways. Bring a pan of lightly salted water to the boil. Add the onions and simmer for 2 minutes. Remove the onion wedges with a slotted spoon and set aside. Add the sugar snap peas to the boiling water and simmer for 1 minute. Tip into a colander and leave to drain.

3 Preheat the oven to 200°C/400°F/Gas 6 and place a roasting pan in the oven to heat. Spiralize the potatoes and beetroot using the slicing blade to make concertina-type ribbons. Mix together the oil and fruit juice in a bowl and season with a little salt and pepper, add the potato and beetroot ribbons and softened onions, and use your hands to lightly coat the mixture. Tip into the roasting pan and roast for 15–18 minutes, turning the vegetables once or twice, so that they cook evenly.

4 Meanwhile, heat a small non-stick frying pan or skillet over a high heat until hot. Remove the duck breasts from the marinade (there will only be a spoonful or two, but reserve it for later) and pat dry with kitchen paper. Add to the pan, skin-side down, and fry for 2 minutes. Turn the duck breasts over and cook for about 30 seconds to brown and seal the underside of the duck.

5 Arrange the duck, skin-side up on a wire rack set over a roasting pan, then roast in the oven for 8–10 minutes, depending on how well you like your duck cooked. Remove from the oven, take off the skin and discard, and baste the duck with the reserved marinade. Add the sugar snap peas to the roasted vegetables and mix together. Return the duck and vegetables to the oven for a further 2–3 minutes.

6 Thinly slice the duck breasts and add to the vegetables. Gently toss everything together, then divide between warmed plates and serve straight away.

DF **GF**

Serves 4
3 large boneless duck breasts
2cm/¾in piece fresh root ginger, peeled and grated
10ml/2 tsp toasted sesame oil
5ml/1 tsp ground cinnamon
15ml/1 tbsp dark soy sauce
15ml/1 tbsp rice wine or dry sherry
5ml/1 tsp light muscovado (brown) sugar
4 small red onions, peeled
175g/6oz sugar snap peas or mangetouts (snow peas)
2 medium potatoes, about 350g/ 12oz, peeled
3 medium beetroot (beet), about 300g/10oz, peeled
30ml/2 tbsp coconut or sunflower oil
15ml/1 tbsp apple or orange juice
Salt and ground black pepper

FISH MAINS

Delicious and healthy, fish and shellfish are a great source of protein and minerals, including zinc, iron, potassium and iodine. While white fish is low in fat, oily fish such as salmon and trout are a major source of polyunsaturated fatty acids such as omega-3. Fish cooks relatively quickly, so is ideal for combining with spiralized vegetables. Incredibly versatile, it can be cooked in all manner of ways, to make both light and hearty dishes. Try smoked trout roulade for sophisticated summer dining or cod with chorizo and chilli for winter comfort.

Chorizo oil is whisked with lemon juice and brushed over cod fillets to add flavour and keep them succulent during cooking. They are served on a bed of dark green Puy lentils which have a unique peppery flavour. Spiralized courgettes and carrots add texture and colour to the finished dish which is perfect served with some warm crusty bread.

Cod with chorizo and spiralized vegetable lentils

 DF **GF**

Serves 4

1 onion, peeled
1 large carrot, peeled
1 large courgette (zucchini), about 250g/9oz
15ml/1 tbsp olive oil
1 fresh red chilli, seeded and finely chopped
175g/6oz/1 cup Puy lentils, rinsed and drained
750ml/1½ pints/3 cups vegetable stock
1 bay leaf
75g/3oz chorizo, cut into cubes slightly smaller than 1cm/½in
Juice of 1 lemon
4 cod fillet steaks, about 150g/5oz each
Salt and ground black pepper

1 Spiralize the onion, carrot and courgette using the medium (3mm/⅛in) spiralizer noodle blade. Cut them into shorter lengths, about 7.5cm/3in.

2 Heat the oil in a pan, add the onion and chilli and cook gently for 3 minutes. Add the lentils, vegetable stock and bay leaf and bring to the boil. Lower the heat and simmer for 15 minutes. Stir in the carrots and cook for a further minute, then stir in the courgettes and cook for 3 minutes or until the lentils and vegetables are tender. Most of the stock should have been absorbed, but if there is some remaining liquid, drain off the excess.

3 Meanwhile, cook the chorizo in a dry non-stick frying pan or skillet over a medium heat for 4–5 minutes or until lightly browned and there is plenty of oil from the chorizo in the pan. Remove the chorizo with a slotted spoon and transfer to a plate, leaving the oil behind in the pan.

4 Tip most of the oil into a small bowl, leaving about 10ml/2 tsp in the pan. Whisk the lemon juice with the chorizo oil and season with salt and pepper. Brush the skinless side of the cod with the oil and lemon mixture.

5 Place the cod, skin-side down in the pan. Cook over a moderate heat until the skin is crispy and the flesh is opaque and cooked through. Turn over the fish and cook for a further minute to lightly brown the top. At the same time, return the chorizo to the pan and cook for a minute to warm through.

6 Spoon the lentil and vegetable mixture on to warmed plates and top each with a piece of cod and a scattering of chorizo. Serve straight away.

Simple grilled sea bass is paired with crispy potato and fennel rosti and finished with a zesty lime and caper dressing which is drizzled over the fish after cooking. Serve with a baby leaf salad or a vegetable such as steamed kale or tenderstem broccoli, if you like.

Grilled sea bass with spiralized fennel potato rosti

1 Check the sea bass fillets and remove any small bones with tweezers. Trim and cut each fillet in half. Brush both sides with 15ml/1 tbsp olive oil and lightly season the skinless side with salt and ground black pepper. Place the fish skin-side up on a grill or broiling pan lined with oiled foil.

2 Spiralize the potatoes using the medium (3mm/⅛in) spiralizer noodle blade. Using your hands, squeeze out as much juice as possible, then put the potatoes in a bowl. Slice the fennel using the spiralizer slicing blade, then add to the potatoes, lightly season with salt and pepper and mix together. Add the beaten egg and mix again, then shape into 8 rounds, each about 8cm/3in across.

3 Heat the oil in a large non-stick frying pan and cook the rosti over a medium heat for 4–5 minutes on each side, until golden and cooked through.

4 While the rosti are cooking, preheat the grill or broiler to high. To make the dressing, put the oil, lime zest and juice and capers in a small bowl and whisk together with a fork.

5 Grill or broil the sea bass fillets for 4–6 minutes without turning, depending on thickness, until the skin is crisp and the flesh is opaque and flakes easily. Watch carefully, as the skin burns quickly.

6 Arrange the rosti on warmed plates and top with the sea bass fillets. Drizzle the lime and caper dressing over the fish and serve with a baby leaf salad. Garnish with lime wedges.

Sometimes simplicity is best when it comes to serving fish and the delicate flavour of seabass needs nothing more than a light dressing. Crisp vegetable rosti are the perfect partner

Serves 4
4 x 150g/5oz sea bass fillets
15ml/1 tbsp olive oil
Salt and ground black pepper
Wedges of lime, to garnish
Baby leaf salad, to serve

For the rosti:
2 large waxy potatoes, about 500g/
 1¼lb, peeled
2 fennel bulbs
1 egg, lightly beaten
15ml/1 tbsp olive oil

For the lime and caper dressing:
15ml/1 tbsp olive oil
Zest of ½ and juice of 1 lime
30ml/2 tsp capers, drained

143

Spiralized carrots give this light fluffy roulade a subtle flavour and stunning golden colour. It's filled with tender flakes of smoked trout, cucumber, fresh dill and crème fraîche and is great for summer entertaining as it can be made in advance. Serve with a baby leaf or rocket salad and wedges of fresh lime or lemon to squeeze over.

Smoked trout and spiralized carrot roulade

Serves 4–6
2 large carrots, about 225g/8oz
25g/1oz/2 tbsp butter or margarine
25g/1oz/¼ cup plain (all-purpose) flour
150ml/¼ pint/⅔ cup milk
3 large eggs, separated
45ml/3 tbsp chopped fresh dill
½ cucumber
150ml/¼ pint/⅔ cup crème fraîche
115g/4oz smoked trout, chopped
Salt and ground black pepper

1 Lightly oil a 33 x 28cm/13 x 11in Swiss or jelly roll tin or pan and line with baking parchment. Spiralize the carrots using the fine (2mm/¹⁄₁₂in) noodle blade. Cut into shorter lengths around 7.5cm/3in.

2 Preheat the oven to 180°C/350°F/Gas 4. Melt the butter in a heavy pan. Sprinkle over the flour and stir over a low heat to make a thick paste. Gradually stir in the milk, then add the spiralized carrots. Bring to the boil and simmer over a low heat for 1–2 minutes until the sauce thickens. Remove from the heat and allow to cool for a few minutes.

3 Stir the egg yolks and chopped dill into the sauce. Whisk the egg whites in a large clean bowl, until stiff and fold into the mixture, one third at a time. Spoon into the prepared tin and bake for 12–15 minutes, until slightly risen and firm to the touch. Place the tin on a wire rack and cover with a clean dish towel.

4 While the roulade is cooking and cooling, trim the ends of the cucumber straight, then make a lengthways cut from one side through to the middle (this will enable you to make single slices rather than joined concertina slices). Slice the cucumber using the spiralizer slicing blade. Place the slices in a colander and lightly sprinkle with salt. Leave for 15 minutes to draw out some of the juices, then thoroughly rinse under cold running water and pat dry on kitchen paper.

5 Mix together the crème fraîche and smoked trout. Tip out the roulade on to a sheet of baking parchment and carefully peel away the lining paper. Spread evenly with the smoked trout mixture, then arrange the cucumber slices on top in a single layer. Roll up from one of the short ends and place on a board seam-side down. Cover with clear film or plastic wrap and keep in the refrigerator, before slicing with a large serrated knife to serve.

This Malaysian seafood noodle dish contains spiralized fennel and mooli which soak up all the delicious spicy flavours. Traditionally it is very hot, but this is a much milder version made with smooth thick creamy coconut milk to mellow the spices.

Spiralized seafood laksa

1 Put the chillies, garlic, paprika, ginger and shallots in a small food processor or spice grinder. Remove the leaves from the coriander, finely chop and reserve. Roughly chop the stems and add to the food processor with 30ml/2 tbsp water. Blend to a paste, stopping halfway through and scraping down the sides.

2 Slice the fennel using the spiralizer slicing blade, then spiralize the mooli using the fine (2mm/¹⁄₁₂in) noodle blade.

3 Heat the oil in a large pan, add the fennel and cook for 3–4 minutes or until just beginning to colour. Add the spice paste and stir-fry for 2 minutes. Gradually, pour in the fish or vegetable stock, stirring to blend, and bring to the boil. Simmer uncovered for 7–8 minutes.

4 Add the coconut milk, lime juice and fish sauce and bring to the boil. Meanwhile, remove the basil leaves from the stems, tearing the larger leaves into smaller pieces.

5 Add the spiralized mooli noodles to the pan, bring back to the boil, then add the fish and gently simmer for 2 minutes. Add the prawns and simmer for a further 1½–2 minutes. Gently simmer until the fish is tender and opaque and the prawns are pink and just cooked through.

6 Reserve a few basil leaves as a garnish, then stir the rest with the chopped fresh coriander leaves into the soup. Ladle into warmed bowls, twirling the noodles into 'nests', and serve garnished with the basil leaves.

DF **GF**

Serves 4
2 fresh red chillies, seeded
2 garlic cloves, peeled
5ml/1 tsp ground paprika
2cm/¾in piece fresh ginger, peeled and
   roughly chopped
2 shallots, peeled and roughly chopped
25g/1oz fresh coriander (cilantro)
1 fennel bulb
1 mooli (daikon)
15ml/1 tbsp coconut or groundnut
   (peanut) oil
300ml/½ pint/1¼ cups fish or
   vegetable stock
400ml/14fl oz/1⅔ cup canned
   coconut milk
Juice of 1 lime
30ml/2 tbsp Thai fish sauce (nam pla)
Small bunch fresh basil
350g/12oz firm white fish such as
   monkfish or halibut, cut into
   2cm/¾in chunks
350g/12oz large raw prawns (shrimp),
   shelled and deveined

Here fresh salmon is flavoured with spring onions, mustard, honey and lemon, then shaped into patties and baked. After cooking, the patties are served between two crispy potato cakes with fresh peppery watercress. Classic celeriac remoulade with its crunchy texture and subtle celery-like texture makes a great accompaniment.

Salmon and spiralized potato cakes with celeriac

Serves 2

For the potato patties:
2 medium potatoes, about 400g/
  14oz, peeled
15ml/1 tbsp olive oil
1 clove garlic, crushed
1 egg, lightly beaten
Salt and ground black pepper

For the salmon burgers:
225g/8oz skinless, boneless
  salmon fillets
5ml/1 tsp honey
Juice of ½ lemon
4 spring onions (scallions), finely sliced
25g/1oz watercress sprigs, large
  stalks removed

For the celeriac remoulade:
1 small or medium celeriac
Juice of 1 lemon
30ml/2 tbsp mayonnaise
60ml/4 tbsp crème fraîche
5ml/1 tsp wholegrain mustard

1 Spiralize the potatoes, using the fine (2mm/¹⁄₁₂in) noodle spiralizer blade. Heat the oil in a large non-stick frying pan or skillet, add the noodles and cook over a medium-low heat for 6–7 minutes, stirring frequently until the noodles have softened and coloured a little. Add the garlic and season with salt and pepper, then cook for a further minute. Tip the noodles into a bowl and leave until cool enough to handle.

2 Add the beaten egg and stir to coat all the noodles. Take four 10cm/4in ramekins, custard cups or small dishes and divide the noodles between them; they should be about half full. Take a clean can (baked beans, soup, tomatoes, for example) and firmly press down the noodles to flatten and level the surface. Chill the dishes in the refrigerator for about 20 minutes.

3 Preheat the oven to 200°C/400°F/Gas 6. Line a baking sheet with baking parchment. Check the salmon for bones and trim if necessary. Cut into chunks and put in a food processor with the honey, lemon juice and a little salt and pepper.

4 Process the salmon mixture for a few seconds until roughly chopped, then add the sliced spring onions and pulse the mixture until you have a lumpy paste; it should still have small chunks of salmon, but should hold together. Shape the mixture into two round fish cakes, each very slightly larger than 10cm/4in diameter.

5 Run a knife around the edge of the ramekins, cups or dishes and shake the potato cakes out on to the baking sheet. Add the two salmon fishcakes. Bake for 15 minutes or until the potato cakes are browned and the salmon fishcakes are cooked through (the middle should be the same whitish-pink colour as the outside).

6 While the fishcakes and potato cakes are baking, make the celeriac remoulade. Spiralize the celeriac with the medium (3mm/¹⁄₈in) spiralizer noodle blade and cut the noodles into 7.5cm/3in lengths. Immediately toss with the lemon juice to prevent it discoloring. Mix the mayonnaise, crème fraîche and mustard together in a bowl, add the celeriac and season with salt and pepper. Mix well.

7 Place a potato cake on a warmed plate and top with half the watercress sprigs. Top with a salmon fishcake then with a second potato cake, so that the fishcake is sandwiched between two potato cakes, burger style. Repeat with the remaining potato cakes, watercress and salmon fishcake on a second plate. Serve with the celeriac remoulade.

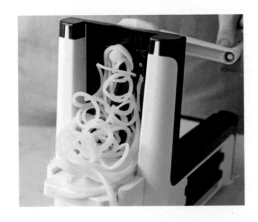

Baking fish 'en papillote' (enclosing in a bag made from baking parchment) is a simple, trouble-free way to cook fish. It prevents steam from escaping, so allows the fish to cook gently and stay moist. Fine spiralized vegetables are perfect for this dish, as they cook really quickly. This is a meal in itself, but is good served with rice or couscous.

Tuna spiralizer Niçoise

1 Cut out 4 circles of baking parchment of about 30cm/12in diameter. Slice the fennel using the spiralizer slicing blade and spiralize the courgette using the fine (2mm/1⁄12in) spiralizer noodle blade.

2 Heat 15ml/1 tbsp of the oil in a large non-stick frying pan, skillet or wok, add the fennel slices and cook for 2 minutes, then add the spiralized courgette and cook for a further minute, stirring frequently, to soften the vegetables slightly. Turn off the heat, stir in the lemon juice and season with salt and pepper.

3 Put the plum tomatoes in a small heatproof bowl and pour over enough boiling water to cover. Leave for 45 seconds to 1 minute, or until the skins start to split and peel, then remove with a slotted spoon, rinse under cold water and peel off the skins. Cut each tomato into 6 wedges.

4 Preheat the oven to 200°C/400°F/Gas 6. Fold the paper circles in half, then open out. Divide the courgette, fennel, tomato and olives between them, piling on to one half of the paper circle and leaving a 5cm/2in border around the edge.

5 Brush a ridged frying pan with the remaining 15ml/1 tbsp oil and heat until very hot. Sear the tuna steaks on one side for about 1 minute so that you have lightly charred lines on the top (you can leave this step out if you prefer and oven-cook the fish for an extra 1–2 minutes instead). Place on top of the vegetables, seared-side up, then sprinkle with the thyme.

6 Fold the other half of the paper circle over the fish and vegetables and fold over and pleat around the edge to make parcels. Put on a baking sheet and cook in the oven for 7 minutes or until the fish is just cooked; it will be slightly pink in the centre. If you prefer tuna well done, cook for 1–2 minutes longer.

DF · GF · P

Serves 4
2 fennel bulbs
1 large courgette (zucchini), about 250g/9oz
30ml/2 tbsp olive oil
15ml/1 tbsp lemon juice
2 plum tomatoes
4 tuna steaks, 2cm/3⁄4in thick, about 150g/5oz each
12 pitted olives, quartered lengthways
10ml/2 tsp chopped fresh thyme leaves
Salt and ground black pepper

This classic Italian dish is usually made with pasta, but here courgette noodles makes it a much lower carbohydrate dish. Most of the ingredients for the sauce should hopefully be found in your store cupboard; if not, it's well-worth stocking up on them, as this is a great stand-by supper dish and tastes every bit as good as it looks.

Courgetti alla puttanesca

Serves 4
15ml/1 tbsp, plus 5ml/1 tsp olive oil
2 cloves garlic, finely chopped
1 small red chilli, finely chopped
50g/2oz can anchovy fillets, drained
  and chopped
16 pitted black olives, sliced in half
15ml/1 tbsp capers, drained
200g/7oz can chopped tomatoes
2.5ml/½ tsp dried oregano
45ml/3 tbsp chopped fresh parsley
Ground black pepper
4 large courgettes (zucchini), about
  1kg/2¼lb

1 Heat 15ml/1 tbsp of the oil in a pan and add the garlic, chilli and anchovy fillets. Fry for 3–4 minutes, stirring frequently until the garlic is turning golden, crushing the anchovies to a paste as you stir.

2 Add the olives and capers and stir-fry for a few more seconds, then stir in the tomatoes and oregano. Bring to the boil, then lower the heat, cover and simmer for 15 minutes. Stir in the parsley and season the sauce with ground black pepper (don't add salt as the anchovies will be salty already). Cover and gently simmer for a further 5 minutes.

3 While the sauce is cooking, spiralize the courgettes using the 2mm/¹⁄₁₂in (fine) noodle blade. Heat the remaining 5ml/1 tsp olive oil in a large non-stick frying pan, skillet or wok. Add the courgette noodles and cook over a medium-high heat for 2–3 minutes, stirring frequently, until just tender.

4 Pour the sauce over the courgettes and cook, stirring frequently for a further minute, so that the noodles absorb the flavours of the sauce. If you find the sauce a little dry (this will depend on the water content of the courgettes), add a few spoonfuls of well-flavoured vegetable stock. Serve immediately.

A traditional dish with a new twist; rich, warming and comforting noodles with a fraction of the calorie content

These popular Oriental-style parcels are given a new twist and are made with filo pastry and oven-baked rather than deep-fried. Fine spiralized carrots and courgettes make a tempting filling together with low-fat prawns. Spiralized mooli salad (see page 92) would make an excellent accompaniment.

Crispy prawn spring rolls

1 Remove the filo pastry from the refrigerator and leave it, still wrapped, at room temperature for about 10 minutes (this will help stop it cracking when unrolling). Spiralize the courgette and carrot using the fine (2mm/1/12in) spiralizer noodle blade. Cut into shorter lengths about 5cm/2in long. Trim the spring onions and cut each in half widthways, then cut into fine matchstick strips, lengthways.

2 Heat 10ml/2 tsp of the groundnut or sunflower oil and the sesame oil in a large non-stick frying pan, skillet or wok and add the courgette and carrot. Cook over a moderate heat for 3 minutes, stirring frequently. Add the spring onions, ginger and beansprouts and cook for a further 2 minutes, until the vegetables are just tender.

3 Sprinkle over the soy sauce and sherry and turn up the heat a little. Cook for a further minute, stirring all the time until the vegetable juices have evaporated (the mixture should be fairly dry or the spring rolls will be soggy). Turn off the heat and leave to cool, stirring occasionally to allow the steam to escape, then stir in the prawns.

4 Preheat the oven to 190°C/375°F/Gas 5. Unroll the filo pastry and trim the sheets into 20cm/8in squares. Lightly brush 3 squares with oil, then cover with the remaining 3 squares. Cut each into four to give 12 squares and carefully cover with a piece of clear film, plastic wrap or a damp clean dish towel to stop the pastry drying out.

5 Spoon a heaped tablespoon of filling along one edge of each pastry square, leaving a 1cm/1/2in border. Tuck the pastry over the filling at the sides and roll up to encase the filling, lightly oiling the end to seal. Place seam-side down on a baking sheet lined with baking parchment. Make all the spring rolls in the same way until all the filling and pastry is used up, then lightly brush the rolls with the remaining oil.

6 Bake the spring rolls for 12–15 minutes, until the pastry is dark golden and crisp. Transfer to a wire rack and allow the rolls to cool slightly before serving.

Cook's tip
Drain the prawns well on kitchen paper and gently blot them to soak up any liquid before adding to the vegetable mixture.

Serves 4 (makes 12 rolls)
6 sheets filo pastry, about 175g/6oz
1 large courgette (zucchini), about 250g/9oz
1 large carrot
4 spring onions (scallions)
About 30ml/2 tbsp groundnut (peanut) or sunflower oil
5ml/1 tsp sesame oil
2cm/3/4in piece fresh root ginger, peeled and grated
115g/4oz beansprouts
30ml/2 tbsp dark soy sauce
15ml/1 tbsp dry sherry
115g/4oz small prawns (shrimp), defrosted if frozen

Serve these crisp little spring rolls packed with juicy vegetables with sweet chilli sauce or soy sauce to dip

This warm salad is quick and simple to make using a bag of mixed ready-prepared seafood. The courgette 'rice' and spiralized pepper noodles should be tender, but still with a little crunch, and the seafood just warmed through in the sun-dried tomato dressing.

Warm courgette rice and pepper noodle salad with seafood

Serves 4

3 large courgettes (zucchini), about 800g/1¾lb
1 red (bell) pepper
1 yellow (bell) pepper
1 fennel bulb, about 225g/8oz
45ml/3 tbsp olive oil
1 sheet nori seaweed
Juice of 1 lemon
15ml/1 tbsp finely chopped sun-dried tomatoes packed in oil
1 packet frozen mixed seafood about 400g/14oz, thawed and drained
Salt and ground black pepper

1 Spiralize the courgettes using the fine (2mm/¹⁄₁₂in) spiralizer noodle blade. Snip the noodles into shorter lengths with kitchen scissors and put in a food processor (you may need to do this in two batches, depending on the capacity of your food processor). Pulse for a few seconds until the noodles are chopped into rice-sized pieces.

2 Spiralize the red and yellow peppers using the fine (2mm¹⁄₁₂in) noodle blade and cut into 10cm/4in lengths with clean kitchen scissors. Slice the fennel using the spiralizer slicing blade.

3 Heat 15ml/1 tbsp of the oil in a large non-stick frying pan, skillet or wok. Add the courgette 'rice' and stir-fry for 3–4 minutes or until the courgettes are just tender. Tip into a fine-holed colander or large sieve or strainer and leave any juices to drain over the sink. Cover the colander with a lid to keep warm.

4 Add a further 15ml/1 tbsp of the oil to the pan, add the spiralized peppers and fennel and stir-fry for 3–4 minutes or until just tender. Tip into the colander on top of the courgette rice.

5 Toast the sheet of seaweed, by briefly holding over the flame of a gas burner for a few seconds on each side until it darkens slightly and becomes crisp. Snip into fine strips with kitchen scissors and set aside.

6 Gently heat the remaining 15ml/1 tbsp oil in the pan with the lemon juice, sun-dried tomatoes, salt and pepper. Add the seafood and stir to coat in the dressing. Return the courgette rice, peppers and fennel to the pan and mix together over a low heat until warmed through. Tip on to a serving plate or individual bowls and scatter over the toasted nori strips.

VEGETARIAN

In this chapter all kinds of spiralized vegetables take the starring role, bringing exciting flavours and textures to every meal. Packed with vitamins, minerals, protective compounds and fibre, many recipes also include beans or grains to add protein. Try summer frittata with spiralized salsa or courgetti Genovese with a classic pesto sauce. And if you are looking for simple spiralized side dishes to serve with a main course, you'll find them here. Curly fries are quick and easy to bake in the oven, or try temping potato latkes or baked shoestring onions to serve with hot foods or a marinated cucumber salad to complement cold ones.

Although avocados have a high fat content, like nuts most of the fat is monounsaturated and therefore good for you. In addition, they are a great source of the antioxidant vitamin E, which helps slow the ageing process. Turn them into a creamy sauce and serve over sautéed spiralized courgette noodles, for a quick lunch or supper dish.

Coodles with creamy avocado sauce

1 Spiralize the courgettes using the fine (2mm/¹⁄₁₂in) spiralizer noodle blade. Break or cut into slightly shorter more manageable lengths.

2 Halve and remove the stones or pits from the avocados. Roughly dice the flesh and put in a food processor with 15ml/1 tbsp of the oil, lemon juice, water, salt and pepper. Blend to a smooth sauce, adding a little more lemon juice if you prefer a sharper flavour.

3 Heat the remaining oil in a large non-stick frying pan, skillet or wok. Add the courgette noodles and stir-fry over a moderate heat for 2–4 minutes or until the courgettes are just tender or cooked to your liking. Turn up the heat a little for the last 30 seconds of cooking to allow juices from the courgettes to evaporate (as these will dilute the sauce).

4 Pour most of the avocado sauce over the courgette noodles and stir to coat. Divide between warmed bowls, drizzle over the remaining sauce and serve straight away.

Cook's tip
You can also serve this sauce with raw spiralized courgettes or other raw or cooked vegetable noodles.

This smooth avocado sauce can be made in a food processor in minutes and is the perfect partner to low-calorie courgette noodles

Serves 4
4 large courgettes (zucchini)
2 medium ripe avocados
30ml/2 tbsp olive oil
15ml/1 tbsp lemon juice
15ml/1 tbsp water
Salt and ground black pepper

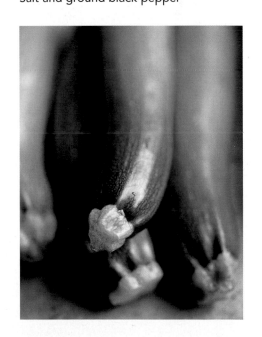

'Arrabbiata' is the Italian word for 'angry' and refers to the spiciness of this deliciously simple tomato and chilli sauce. Traditionally it is served with chunky pasta such as penne, but spiralized courgette concertina ribbons make a superb low-carbohydrate alternative. You can buy chilli oil, but it's really simple to make your own (see cook's tip).

Courgette ribbons with arrabbiata sauce

VT **GF** (vegan and dairy-free if served without Parmesan)

Serves 4
45ml/3 tbsp chilli oil
2 cloves garlic, peeled and
   finely chopped
5ml/1 tsp fennel seeds
400g/14oz can chopped tomatoes
120ml/4fl oz/½ cup red wine or
   vegetable stock
1 bay leaf
4 large courgettes (zucchini), ideally
   2 green and 2 yellow, about 1kg/2¼lb
Salt and ground black pepper
Parmesan (vegetarian) shavings,
   to serve (optional)

1 Heat 30ml/2 tbsp of the chilli oil in a medium pan, add the garlic and fennel and cook over a low heat for 1–2 minutes until the garlic just starts to colour. Add the tomatoes, red wine or vegetable stock and bay leaf to the pan and bring to the boil. Reduce the heat and simmer uncovered for 15–20 minutes or until the sauce has reduced and is fairly thick. Season to taste with salt and ground black pepper

2 Meanwhile, spiralize the courgettes using the slicing blade of the spiralizer to create courgette ribbons. When the sauce is nearly ready, heat the remaining 15ml/1 tbsp chilli oil in a large non-stick frying pan, skillet or wok. Add the courgette ribbons and stir-fry over a moderate heat for 3–4 minutes until the courgettes are just tender. Turn up the heat a little for the last minute of cooking to allow any juices from the courgettes to evaporate (as these may dilute the sauce).

3 Pour the tomato sauce over the courgettes and stir-fry for a further minute to allow the courgette ribbons to soak up the flavour of the sauce. Serve in warmed pasta bowls, scattered with Parmesan shavings, if liked.

Cook's tip
To make chilli oil, halve 3 fresh, moderately hot red chillies and put in a small pan with a bay leaf and 2 cloves peeled garlic. Pour over 150ml/¼ pint/⅔ cup olive oil. Place on a very low heat and gently warm for 20 minutes or until the garlic and chillies are very soft (if the oil starts to get too hot during this time, turn off the heat for a few minutes). Leave to cool, then strain through a muslin- or cheesecloth-lined sieve, strainer or coffee filter paper into a jug or pitcher. Pour the oil into a clean bottle or jam jar, discarding the chillies, bay leaf and garlic. Store in the refrigerator for up to 2 months.

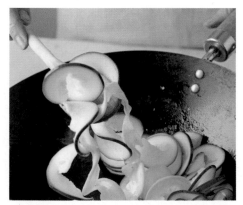

Here an ordinary omelette is turned into something special. Packed with colourful stir-fried spiralized vegetables, eggs are mixed with a little cornflour to make the individual omelettes easier to fold. You can vary the filling according to your personal taste, or depending on the leftover bits and pieces of vegetables you may have in the refrigerator.

Thai spiralized vegetable omelette

1 Spiralize the carrot and mooli using the fine (2mm/1⁄12in) spiralizer noodle blade. Snip into slightly shorter lengths with clean kitchen scissors. Slice the cabbage and pepper with the spiralizer slicing blade.

2 Lightly beat the eggs in a jug or pitcher to break up the yolks, then sprinkle over the cornflour and add 10ml/2 tsp of the soy sauce. Whisk together until mixed.

3 Heat 5ml/1 tsp of the sunflower oil in a 20cm/8in non-stick omelette pan over a moderate heat. Pour in a quarter of the egg mixture and gently swirl in the pan to spread out into an even layer. Cook for about 2 minutes or until lightly set and golden brown underneath. Slide the omelette out of the pan on to a warmed plate and cover with foil. Make the remaining three omelettes in the same way.

4 While the omelettes are cooking, heat the remaining 10ml/2 tsp sunflower oil and sesame oil in a large frying pan, skillet or wok. Add the mushrooms and stir-fry for 1 minute, then add the green pepper and cabbage and cook for a further minute.

5 Stir in the carrot and mooli noodles and 30ml/2 tbsp water to create a little steam and stop the vegetables sticking to the pan. Continue stir-frying for 2–3 minutes, or until the vegetables are tender but still have a slightly crisp texture. Add the remaining 20ml/4 tsp soy sauce and rice vinegar, then squeeze in the juices from the grated ginger and cook for a few more seconds, stirring to coat all the vegetables.

6 Divide the vegetables between the omelettes on warmed plates and fold them over in half to enclose the mixture. Serve immediately.

 VT

Serves 4
1 large carrot, peeled
½ large mooli (daikon), peeled
175g/6oz white cabbage
1 small green (bell) pepper, seeded and thinly sliced
8 eggs
20ml/4 tsp cornflour (cornstarch)
30ml/2 tbsp light soy sauce
30ml/2 tbsp sunflower oil
5ml/1 tsp sesame oil
115g/4oz mushrooms, thinly sliced
10ml/2 tsp rice vinegar
2cm/¾in fresh root ginger, peeled and grated

This Italian dish is made with classic pesto sauce: a blend of pine nuts, olive oil, fresh basil, garlic and Parmesan, a wonderful mix of fragrant flavours. There's nothing quite like the taste of home-made, but if you are too busy to make your own, use a good-quality shop-bought jar; it's a great ingredient to keep in the cupboard as a stand-by.

Courgetti Genovese

Serves 4

3 large courgettes (zucchini), preferably a mixture of green and yellow, about 800g/1¾lb
1 large carrot
1 medium waxy potato, peeled and cut into 1cm/¾in cubes
Sprigs of fresh basil, to garnish

For the pesto sauce:
Leaves from a large bunch of basil, about 40g/1½oz
2 garlic cloves, peeled
50g/2oz/½ cup pine nuts
120ml/4fl oz/½ cup olive oil
25g/1oz/¼ cup freshly grated vegetarian Parmesan
10ml/2 tsp fresh lemon juice
Salt and ground black pepper

Variations

For rocket (arugula) pesto, replace the basil with rocket leaves and 30ml/2 tbsp roughly chopped fresh parsley leaves.

For mint and almond pesto, replace the basil with 25g/1oz fresh mint leaves and 25g/1oz flat-leaf parsley leaves. Use blanched almonds instead of the pine nuts. When cooking the vegetables, use 75g/3oz/½ cup defrosted petit pois instead of the spiralized carrot.

1 To make the pesto, roughly tear the basil leaves and place in a mortar with the garlic, pine nuts and 30ml/2 tbsp of the oil. Pound with a pestle into a paste. Alternatively, place the ingredients in a food processor and blend until fairly smooth.

2 Reserve 30ml/2 tbsp of the oil and gradually work the rest into the basil mixture (if you are using a food processor, pour in through the feed tube in a thin drizzle). Transfer to a bowl and stir in the Parmesan and lemon juice. Season to taste with salt and pepper.

3 Spiralize the courgettes and carrot using the 3mm/⅛in (medium) spiralizer noodle blade.

4 Bring a large pan of lightly salted water to the boil. Add the potato cubes, bring back to the boil and simmer, covered for 7 minutes. Add the carrot noodles and when the water comes back to the boil, add the courgette noodles. Cook for a further 3 minutes or until all the noodles are tender.

5 Tip into a colander and drain thoroughly, shaking gently for a minute to allow some of the steam to evaporate. Tip the vegetables back into the pan and heat gently for a few seconds to evaporate any juices which leak from the courgettes. Spoon over half of the pesto sauce, stir to coat all the vegetables, then serve straight away on warm plates. Garnish with basil sprigs.

6 Spoon the remaining pesto into a clean glass jar and top with the reserved 30ml/2 tbsp olive oil (this will help preserve it). Store in the refrigerator for up to 2 weeks.

Much more substantial than an omelette, this easy oven-baked frittata contains spiralized turnips, onions and sweet potato together with goat's cheese. It may sound an unusual combination but the slightly peppery flavour of the turnips works well with the sweetness of the other vegetables and the tangy creaminess of the cheese.

Summer frittata with spiralized salsa

1 For the onion, cucumber and tomato salsa, slice the red onions using the spiralizer slicing blade. Set aside half the sliced onion for the frittata, then chop the remaining slices into slightly smaller pieces. Whisk together the olive oil and vinegar with ground black pepper in a bowl, add the chopped onions and mix well. Leave to soften and mellow for about 20 minutes.

2 Spiralize the cucumber using the medium (3mm/⅛in) spiralizer noodle blade. Snip into 2.5cm/1in pieces with kitchen scissors. Put the cucumber in a sieve or strainer, sprinkle with a little salt and leave to drain on a plate or over the sink.

3 Spiralize the turnips and sweet potato using the medium (3mm/⅛in) spiralizer noodle blade. Cut the noodles into slightly short lengths. Heat the oil in an ovenproof, non-stick frying pan, add the reserved onions and cook over a low heat for 5 minutes. Add the turnip and sweet potato noodles and garlic and cook for a further 4–5 minutes, stirring frequently until just tender. Spread out the vegetables in an even layer.

4 Preheat the oven to 180°C/350°F/Gas 4. Beat the eggs in a jug or pitcher then stir in the herbs and a little salt and pepper. Pour over the vegetables, cook for 2 minutes over a low heat to set the bottom and sides, then scatter the goat's cheese over the top and cook for a further 2 minutes. Transfer the pan to the oven and cook uncovered for 15–20 minutes or until lightly set and golden-brown.

5 Meanwhile, put the tomatoes in a heatproof bowl and pour over enough boiling water to cover. Leave for about 45 seconds until the skins start to split, then peel off the skins, deseed and dice. Briefly rinse the cucumber under cold running water to remove most of the salt, then pat dry with kitchen paper. Add the tomatoes and cucumber to the onion and dressing mixture and stir together.

6 Remove the frittata from the oven and leave to settle for a few minutes. Cut into wedges, scatter with a few fresh herbs, if liked and serve with the cucumber and tomato salsa.

GF **VT**

Serves 4–6
2 medium red onions, peeled
30ml/2 tbsp olive oil
10ml/2 tsp balsamic vinegar
½ large cucumber
2 medium turnips
1 medium sweet potato,
 about 175g/6oz
1 garlic clove, crushed
8 eggs, lightly beaten
45ml/3 tbsp chopped mixed fresh herbs
 such as flat-leaf parsley, dill and mint,
 plus extra for garnishing
75g/3oz mild, creamy goat's
 cheese, crumbled
225g/8oz plum tomatoes
Salt and ground black pepper

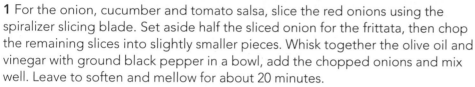
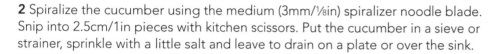

Plantain is too starchy to be successfully boiled as noodles, but it does make an excellent substitute for rice, cooking to a cross between a pilaf and a risotto. Here it is simmered with Caribbean flavourings to make a simple one-pot meal. Black beans add plenty of protein to the dish for vegetarians. Rice and beans is a classic that you must try.

Spicy spiralized plantain rice and beans

1 Peel and spiralize the plantains preferably using the wide (4mm/⅛in) or if your spiralizer doesn't have a wide blade, use the medium (3mm/⅛in) noodle blade. Cut the noodles into shorter lengths and put in a food processor. Pulse until the noodles are chopped into rice-size pieces.

2 Slice the onions using the spiralizer slicing blade. Heat the oil in a large frying pan, skillet or wok and cook the onions over a moderate heat for 5–6 minutes, stirring frequently, until softened. Add the garlic and cook stirring for a few seconds, then stir in the oregano, allspice and chilli flakes.

3 Add the plantain 'rice' to the pan and stir briefly, then add the stock. Simmer for 2 minutes, then stir in the coconut milk and black beans.

4 Bring back to the bowl, then turn the heat to low, cover with a lid and simmer, stirring occasionally for 7–8 minutes or until the 'rice' is tender; take care not to overcook or the plantain will become 'mushy'. Season to taste with salt and pepper and serve on warmed plates.

Cook's tip
If there is a lot of excess liquid towards the end of cooking, remove the lid and turn up the heat a little for the last couple of minutes.

Plantain has a subtle banana flavour but is savoury rather than sweet and is delicious with hot chilli and creamy coconut

V VT DF GF

Serves 4
3 large plantains, about 800g/1¾lb
2 onions, peeled
15ml/1 tbsp sunflower oil
2 cloves garlic, crushed
2.5ml/½ tsp dried oregano
1.5ml/¼ tsp ground allspice
Pinch of dried chilli flakes
350ml/12fl oz/1½ cups well-flavoured
    vegetable stock
250ml/8fl oz/½ cup coconut milk
400g/14oz can black beans, rinsed
    and drained
Salt and ground black pepper

Broccoli stems are often discarded after removing the florets, but have a delicious mild flavour, not unlike asparagus. Although you will only get a small handful of noodles when you spiralize a broccoli stem, it's worth the effort. Here they are combined with butternut squash noodles which add a contrasting colour and taste in a rich blue cheese sauce.

Butternut squash and broccoli noodles

1 Spiralize the butternut squash and broccoli stems using the medium (3mm/⅛in) noodle blade. Bring a large pan of lightly salted water to the boil.

2 Put the pine nuts in a small non-stick frying pan or skillet and gently cook for 3–4 minutes, stirring frequently until just beginning to turn golden. Turn off the heat and leave for a minute or two to cook in the residual heat, then tip on to a cold plate to stop them cooking further.

3 Add the butternut squash and broccoli noodles to the boiling water and simmer for 4–5 minutes or until tender. Alternatively you can cook the noodles in a steamer over boiling water for 6–7 minutes. Tip into a colander and drain.

4 Meanwhile, melt the butter or margarine in a large frying pan, skillet or wok. Add the sage and stir for a few seconds, then turn down the heat to very low.

5 Add the Gorgonzola and mascarpone to the pan. Stir until the cheese starts to melt, then pour in the milk and keep stirring. Season with ground black pepper. Continue to stir over a low heat until the mixture forms a creamy sauce. Do not allow it to boil or it may separate (it doesn't matter if some of the blue cheese hasn't melted).

6 Add the noodles to the pan with most of the toasted pine nuts. Mix well, then twist the noodles into nests and serve in warm bowls. Scatter the remaining pine nuts over the top.

VT **GF**

Serves 4
600g/1lb 6oz piece butternut
   squash, peeled
2 broccoli stems, about 150g/5oz
50g/2oz/½ cup pine nuts
15g/½oz/1 tbsp butter or margarine
5ml/1 tsp finely chopped fresh sage or
   2.5ml/½ tsp dried sage
115g/4oz Gorgonzola cheese, diced
45ml/3 tbsp mascarpone
75ml/5 tbsp milk
Salt and ground black pepper

Rather than throwing away broccoli stems, keep them to make this tasty vegetable noodle dish

Polenta makes a great gluten-free pizza-like base and doesn't need oven-baking. Here it is flavoured with herbs and topped with a garlicky tomato sauce, spiralized vegetable noodles, melting mozzarella and a handful of olives. Serve with a simple mixed leaf salad, if liked.

Mediterranean spiral vegetable and polenta pizza

Serves 4

300g/11oz/3 cups instant polenta
1.2 litres/2 pints/5 cups boiling
   vegetable stock
10ml/2 tsp chopped fresh thyme or
   30ml/2 tbsp chopped fresh parsley
30ml/2 tbsp olive oil
400g/14oz can chopped tomatoes
1 clove garlic, crushed
2 red onions, peeled
2 large courgettes (zucchini), preferably
   1 green, 1 yellow, about 500g/1¼lb
125g/4¼oz packet full or half-fat
   mozzarella cheese, diced, or mini
   mozzarella pearls (balls)
8 black olives, pitted and halved
Salt and ground black pepper

1 Cook the polenta in the boiling vegetable stock in a large pan for about 4–5 minutes, or according to the packet instructions, until thick. Remove from the heat, stir in the herbs and season with salt and ground black pepper. Spoon the polenta into a pizza tin, pan or on to a lightly oiled baking sheet and spread out into a 28–30cm/11–12in round. Brush 1cm/¾in around the edge with 10ml/2 tsp of the olive oil. Set aside.

2 Meanwhile, tip the tomatoes into a wide pan, frying pan or skillet; this will allow them to reduce more quickly. Add the garlic, bring to the boil and simmer over a moderate heat for 5–6 minutes or until very thick.

3 Slice the red onions using the spiralizer slicing blade, then spiralize the courgettes with the slicing blade to create ribbons.

4 Heat the remaining 20ml/4 tsp olive oil in a large frying pan, skillet or wok, add the onions and cook over a low heat for 5–6 minutes or until beginning to soften, stirring frequently. Add the courgettes and cook for 3 minutes or until the vegetables are almost soft, then turn up the heat and cook for a further minute or two to evaporate the juices; the mixture should be quite dry.

5 Preheat the grill or broiler to moderately high. Spread the tomato sauce over the polenta round to within 1cm/¾in of the edge, then top with the onion and courgette mixture. Scatter over the mozzarella and olives. Grill or broil the pizza for 7–8 minutes or until the cheese is golden and bubbling. Cut into wedges and serve.

Glazed spiralized swede with couscous

VT V DF GF

Serves 4

1 large swede (rutabaga), about
   650g/1½lb
30ml/2 tbsp balsamic vinegar
30ml/2 tbsp olive oil
15ml/1 tbsp agave nectar
200g/7oz/generous 1 cup giant couscous
400ml/14fl oz/1¾ cups cold
   vegetable stock
1 sprig fresh thyme, plus a few leaves
   to garnish
50g/2oz baby spinach leaves
Salt and ground black pepper

1 Spiralize the swede using a 4mm/⅙in (wide) spiralizer noodle blade if your machine has one or a 3mm/⅛in (medium) spiralizer blade. Cut into slightly shorter, more manageable lengths, then place in a non-stick roasting pan.

2 Preheat the oven to 180°C/350°F/Mark 4. Whisk the vinegar, 15ml/1 tbsp of the oil, agave nectar, salt and pepper together in a small jug or pitcher. Drizzle over the noodles and mix with your hands to make sure all the noodles are coated. Roast for 15–20 minutes, turning once or twice during cooking. If the noodles start to look a little dry, sprinkle with a spoonful of stock or water.

3 Heat the remaining 15ml/1 tbsp oil in a large pan. Gently fry the couscous for 2 minutes in the oil. Pour in the stock, add the thyme and bring to the boil. Lower the heat, cover and simmer for 12 minutes.

4 Remove the thyme and discard, then add the spinach to the pan (place it on top of the couscous so that it cooks in the steam) and cook for a further 3–4 minutes or until the couscous is cooked and all the stock absorbed and the spinach wilted.

5 Stir the spinach and the roasted swede noodles into the couscous and season to taste with salt and pepper. Spoon on to warmed plates, sprinkled with a few fresh thyme leaves, and serve straight away.

Swede is delicious roasted, and here the spiralized orange noodles are coated with a balsamic glaze then combined with giant couscous and some wilted baby spinach leaves for a colourful supper dish.

If you love pies, but want to avoid eating too much pastry, this bake is a great substitute. Healthy toasted oats are combined with cheese, onions and eggs, then baked until set before turning out.

Spiralized cheese, onion and potato bake

1 Preheat the oven temperature to 180°C/350°F/Gas 4. Grease and line the base of a 20cm/8in cake tin or pan with baking parchment. Spread the oats out on a baking sheet and bake for 10 minutes, until lightly toasted.

2 Spiralize the potatoes using the fine (2mm/¹⁄₁₂in) potato spiralizer noodle blade, then spoon half into the base of the tin, pressing down well. Slice the onions with the spiralizer slicing blade.

3 Heat the oil in a large frying pan, skillet or wok and gently fry the onions for 5–6 minutes, until almost soft, stirring frequently. Snip the remaining spiralized potato noodles into shorter lengths about 10cm/4in and add to the onions with the garlic. Cook for 2 more minutes, then turn off the heat. Add the yeast extract and stir until mixed.

4 Tip the oats into a bowl and add the onion and potato mixture, cheese, parsley, eggs and pepper. Mix well and spoon into the tin, on top of the spiralized potato noodles. Level the top and cover with foil.

5 Bake for 30 minutes until firm and set through. Turn out on to a baking sheet and remove the baking parchment lining. If liked, you can brown the top under a moderately hot grill or broiler. Cut into wedges and serve hot.

Serves 4–6
225g/8oz/2 cups rolled oats
2 medium potatoes, about 350g/12oz
2 medium onions
15ml/1 tbsp sunflower or coconut oil
1 clove garlic, crushed
5ml/1 tsp yeast extract
150g/5oz mature (sharp) Cheddar, coarsely grated
45ml/3 tbsp chopped fresh parsley
2 eggs, lightly beaten
Ground black pepper

Middle-Eastern falafels are protein-packed, but deep-frying makes them a less healthy option. These contain spiralized carrot which adds moistness and texture, and are oven-baked and served with a coriander yogurt dressing for a lower fat, lower calorie meal. Lightly toasted sesame-sprinkled pitta fingers are a tasty addition.

Spiralized falafels and sesame pitta fingers

1 Preheat the oven to 180°C/350°F/Gas 4. Line a baking sheet with baking parchment. Spiralize the carrot using the fine (2mm/¹⁄₁₂in) spiralizer noodle blade. Cut the noodles into shorter lengths about 4cm/1½in with clean kitchen scissors.

2 Tip the chickpeas into a bowl. Add the lemon juice and 15ml/1 tbsp olive oil, then mash with a potato masher until fairly smooth. Add the garlic, cumin and turmeric and season with salt and pepper. Mix briefly, then add the spiralized carrot and mix together well. Alternatively, mix the chickpeas, lemon juice, oil, spices and seasonings together in a food processor, then add the spiralized carrot and pulse for a few seconds to mix.

3 Using damp hands, shape the mixture into 16 balls, then flatten very slightly (so that they won't roll off the sheet) and place on the baking sheet. Bake for 15–18 minutes, or until lightly browned, carefully turning over halfway through cooking time.

4 While the falafels are baking, chop the coriander. Stir together the yogurt and coriander and season to taste with salt and pepper. Spoon into a small bowl.

5 Very lightly brush one side of the pitta breads with half of the remaining oil and place on a baking sheet. Bake in the oven for 4 minutes, then turn over, brush the other side with the rest of the oil and sprinkle over the sesame seeds. Bake for a further 3–4 minutes or until the sesame seeds are golden. Quickly cut the warm pittas into 2cm/¾in fingers using clean kitchen scissors.

6 Serve the falafels hot with the coriander yogurt, pitta fingers and some shredded lettuce and tomatoes.

Cook's tip
Hold each baked pitta with a piece of folded kitchen paper while you cut it, to protect your hand from the heat. Leave the other pittas on the hot baking sheet until you are ready to cut them, as they become crisp as they cool.

Canned ready-cooked chickpeas are combined with warm spices and tender carrots to make these flavoursome falafels; they make a tasty lunch or supper dish

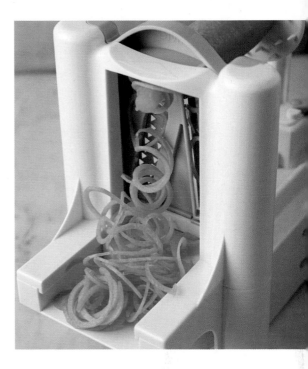

 VT

Serves 4
1 medium-sized carrot (a short fat one!)
400g/14oz can chickpeas, drained and rinsed
15ml/1 tbsp lemon juice
30ml/2 tbsp olive oil
1 clove garlic, crushed
2.5ml/½ tsp ground cumin
1.5ml/¼ tsp ground turmeric
30ml/2 tbsp fresh coriander (cilantro)
150ml/¼ pint/⅔ cup low-fat Greek (US strained plain) yogurt
4 pitta breads, wholemeal (whole-wheat) or white, about 50g/2oz each
45ml/3 tbsp sesame seeds
Salt and ground black pepper
Shredded iceburg lettuce and halved baby plum tomatoes, to serve

This one-pan supper dish of colourful peppers in a rich tomato sauce is based on the classic North African 'chakchouka' and Turkish 'Menemen' which always have the addition of eggs, either scrambled into the mixture or poached, as here.

Spiralized pepper and tomato ragoût

VT **P** **GF** **DF**

Serves 2–4
2 onions, peeled
1 yellow (bell) pepper
1 green (bell) pepper
15ml/1 tbsp olive oil
400g/14oz can chopped tomatoes
60ml/4 tbsp well-flavoured
   vegetable stock
30ml/2 tbsp chopped fresh parsley or
   15ml/1 tbsp chopped fresh oregano
4 eggs

1 Spiralize the onions and peppers using the spiralizer slicing blade. Snip the pepper noodles into more manageable lengths, about 10cm/4in.

2 Heat the oil in a large non-stick frying pan or skillet and gently fry the onions over a low heat for 7–8 minutes, stirring frequently, until soft.

3 Add the pepper noodles and cook for 1 minute, stirring, then add the tomatoes and stock. Let the mixture gently bubble for 3–4 minutes or until the peppers are almost tender and the sauce has reduced and thickened a little. Stir in about half of the chopped parsley or oregano.

4 With a wooden spoon, create 4 hollows in the tomato mixture and crack the eggs into them (it is easier to make the hollows and add the eggs one at a time). Work quickly, or some of the eggs will be cooked sooner than others.

5 Cook for a further 4–6 minutes or until the eggs are lightly set, or cooked to your liking. Sprinkle over the remaining parsley or oregano and serve straight away.

Spiralized mooli noodles with mushrooms

1 Heat the sesame oil and 5ml/1 tsp of the sunflower oil in a non-stick omelette pan. Mix the egg and parsley together with 5ml/1 tsp water and a little salt and pepper and pour into the pan to make a very thin omelette. Cook over a moderate heat for about 1 minute or until set, then turn over and cook for 30 seconds. Slide on to a plate.

2 Spiralize the mooli using the 2mm/¹⁄₁₂in (fine) spiralizer noodle blade. Heat the remaining 15ml/1 tbsp oil in a non-stick large frying pan or wok, add the leeks and mushrooms and cook over a moderate heat for 2–3 minutes, stirring frequently.

3 Add the mooli noodles, garlic and ginger and cook stirring for a further minute. Pour in the stock, add the five-spice powder, cover and steam for 2 minutes, then remove the lid and continue cooking, stirring frequently until most of the stock has evaporated and the noodles and vegetables are tender.

4 Divide between warmed plates, twisting the noodles into nests. Top with any juices. Quickly cut the omelette into thin strips using clean kitchen scissors and pile on top of the noodles and mushrooms. Serve straight away.

Serves 2–4

5ml/1 tsp sesame oil
20ml/4 tsp sunflower oil
1 egg, lightly beaten
15ml/1 tbsp chopped fresh parsley
2 large mooli (daikon)
200g/7oz baby leeks, trimmed and
   sliced lengthways
200g/7oz mixed fresh mushrooms
   (eg shiitake, oyster, chestnut), sliced
2 garlic cloves, peeled and
   finely chopped
5cm/2in piece fresh root ginger, peeled
   and finely chopped
90ml/6 tbsp well-flavoured
   vegetable stock
Pinch of Chinese five-spice powder
Salt and ground black pepper

The mild, slightly peppery flavour of mooli noodles goes well with stronger flavours and will absorb them as it cooks. Here it is combined with a mixture of mushrooms and topped with ribbons of herb-flavoured omelette to make a simple and light supper dish.

The key to making tempura is to use iced water, not to over-mix the batter and to make sure that the oil is the right temperature, so that the batter is crisp, light and not at all greasy. Served with a selection of high-protein dips, this makes a great vegetarian meal.

Spiralized vegetable tempura

Serves 2–4

For the tofu dip:
1 clove garlic, peeled and crushed
175g/6oz silken tofu
15ml/1 tbsp lime juice
5ml/1 tsp sesame oil
10ml/2 tsp tamari (Japanese soy sauce)
2 spring onions (scallions), trimmed
and chopped

For the chilli dip:
45ml/3 tbsp tamari (Japanese soy sauce)
45ml/3 tbsp rice wine or dry sherry
5ml/1 tsp caster (superfine) sugar
5ml/1 tsp finely grated lime zest
Pinch of red chilli flakes

For the tempura:
2 large courgettes (zucchini),
about 500g/1¼lb
1 sweet potato, about 200g/7oz
1 broccoli stem, about 75g/3oz
100g/4oz/1cup plain (all-purpose) flour
15ml/1 tbsp cornflour (cornstarch)
15ml/1 tbsp sesame seeds
Salt and ground black pepper
250ml/8fl oz/1 cup ice-cold sparkling
mineral or soda water
Sunflower oil, for deep-frying

1 For the tofu dip, put the garlic, tofu, lime juice, sesame oil and tamari in a small food processor and blend until smooth. Add the spring onions and blend for about 30 seconds or until they are very finely chopped. Spoon and scrape into a serving bowl and chill until ready to serve.

2 For the chilli dip, whisk all the ingredients together in a small serving bowl with a fork, until the sugar has dissolved. Set aside until ready to serve.

3 Spiralize the courgettes, sweet potato and broccoli stem using the thick (4mm/⅛in) noodle spiralizer blade or medium (3mm/⅛in) if your spiralizer doesn't have a wider noodle blade. Squeeze as much liquid out of the courgette noodles with your hands or blot with kitchen paper. Cut the noodles into 10cm/4in lengths using clean kitchen scissors. Mix the noodles together and twist into small 'nest' shapes ready for dipping and frying.

4 Heat the oven to 150°C/300°F/Gas 2 and cover a baking sheet with kitchen paper. Pour enough oil into a deep-fat fryer, heavy pan or wok to come a third of the way up the pan. Heat to 190°C/375°F or until a cube of bread dropped into the oil rises and sizzles in 30 seconds.

5 When the oil is nearing the correct temperature, mix the flour, cornflour and sesame seeds in a bowl with a little salt and pepper. Add the ice-cold water and mix together briefly to give a slightly lumpy batter. Dip some of the prepared vegetable nests briefly into the batter, one at a time, shake off any excess then carefully add to the hot oil. Don't crowd the pan and have a slotted spoon to hand.

6 Cook the tempura for 3–4 minutes or until golden and crisp. Remove from the oil with a slotted spoon, then drain on the kitchen paper and keep warm in the oven, leaving the door slightly ajar so that they stay crisp. Repeat with the remaining vegetable nests, dipping into the batter just before frying and allowing the oil to come back up to temperature between each batch. Serve straight away with the dips.

Cook's tip
If you prefer you could serve the tempura with minted tzatziki (see page 83) or shop-bought hummus, loosened with a few spoonfuls of yogurt (dairy or soya).

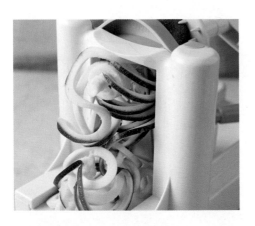

Spiralized curly fries

V **VT** **DF** **GF** **P**

Serves 4

2 large potatoes or sweet potatoes,
    about 450g/1lb
Pinch of salt
5ml/1 tsp mild chilli powder (optional)
10ml/2 tsp ground paprika (optional)
30ml/2 tbsp olive oil

1 Preheat the oven to 200°C/400°F/Gas 6 and line a baking sheet with baking parchment. Spiralize the potatoes using the medium (3mm/⅛in) spiralizer noodle blade. Cut into shorter lengths about 10cm/4in long with clean kitchen scissors.

2 Put the potato noodles in a bowl. Sprinkle with a little salt and chilli powder and paprika, if using, then drizzle over the oil. Mix together with your hands to coat the noodles thoroughly (wash your hands well afterwards if you've used chilli powder).

3 Spread the noodles in an even layer on the baking sheet and bake for 15 minutes. Turn over the noodles and return to the oven for a further 7–10 minutes or until cooked and lightly browned. Sweet potatoes will cook a little faster than ordinary potatoes.

These can be made with either ordinary or sweet potatoes, peeled or with skins left on, and are oven-baked in a small amount of healthy olive oil. You can flavour them with a little chilli powder and paprika or leave them plain. You may need to turn the noodles a couple of times towards the end of cooking to ensure that they cook evenly.

Jewish in origin, this delicious potato dish is crisp on the top and moist and creamy in the middle. It is usually made by grating potatoes which can be a long and tedious chore; a spiralizer creates perfect noodles in a fraction of the time. If the spiralized potatoes are very wet, squeeze out some of the juices, but not too much or the kugel will be dry.

Spiralized potato kugel

1 Spiralize the potatoes and onion using the fine (2mm/¹⁄₁₂in) spiralizer noodle blade. Cut into shorter noodles, about 10cm/4in long with clean kitchen scissors. Squeeze out some of the juices with your hands.

2 Preheat the oven to 200°C/400°F/Gas 6. Whisk the eggs and oil together in a large bowl with a fork. Sprinkle over the flour and season with salt and pepper and whisk again. Add the potatoes and onion and mix well, then tip the mixture into a well-greased ovenproof dish, spread out evenly and push down the noodles with the back of the fork.

3 Put the kugel in the oven and bake for 50 minutes–1 hour or until the mixture is lightly set and the potatoes are tender. Cover the top with foil if the kugel starts to brown too much. Serve hot or warm.

 VT DF

Serves 4
2 large potatoes, about 450g/1lb
1 onion
3 eggs
30ml/2 tbsp sunflower oil
30ml/2 tbsp plain (all-purpose) flour
Salt and ground black pepper

Latkes are usually made in batches in a large frying pan or skillet on the hob. Oven-baking them will ensure they absorb less oil and are all ready at the same time. Squeeze out the excess juices from the spiralized potatoes and onions with your hands, or roll them up in a clean dish towel and wring well.

Spiralized potato latkes

Serves 4
1 large potato, about 250g/9oz
1 small red onion
30ml/2 tbsp plain (all-purpose) flour
1 egg, lightly beaten
Salt and ground black pepper

1 Preheat the oven to 200°C/400°F/Gas 6 and line a baking sheet with baking parchment. Spiralize the potato and red onion using the fine (2mm/¹⁄₁₂in) spiralizer noodle blade. Cut into shorter lengths about 10cm/4in long with clean kitchen scissors, then use your hands to squeeze out as much liquid as possible.

2 Put the vegetable noodles in a bowl and sprinkle over the flour and salt and pepper. Mix well, then add the beaten egg and mix again.

3 Shape into 12 small flat rounds, keeping the edges as neat as possible and the noodles tucked in (or they may burn). Place on the baking sheet, loosely cover with foil and bake for 12 minutes. Turn the latkes over, re-cover with foil and bake for a further 8 minutes, removing the foil for the last 3–4 minutes to allow them to brown.

Spiralized mixed pepper piperade

1 Slice the onion using the spiralizer slicing blade. Spiralize the peppers using the medium (3mm/⅛in) spiralizer noodle blade and cut into 7.5cm/3in lengths. Heat the olive oil in a large non-stick frying pan or skillet and gently cook the onion over a low heat for 6–7 minutes, until almost soft.

2 Add the spiralized peppers to the pan and cook gently for 2–3 minutes. Stir in the crushed garlic clove and the tomatoes. Gently cook for a further 4–5 minutes.

3 Whisk the eggs with 15ml/1 tbsp cold water and season with salt and pepper. Pour the egg mixture over the vegetables and cook for a further 2–3 minutes, stirring occasionally until the consistency of scrambled eggs. Serve on hot wholemeal toast.

Serves 2
1 onion
3 (bell) peppers, any colour, green, orange and red are good
30ml/2 tbsp olive oil
1 garlic clove, crushed
4 tomatoes, peeled, seeded and diced
4 eggs
Hot wholemeal (whole-wheat) toast, to serve
Salt and ground black pepper

This combines scrambled eggs with lots of colourful healthy spiralized peppers, a good source of vitamin C which helps the body absorb iron from the eggs. It makes a great breakfast or light lunch, served with hot wholemeal toast.

Marinated spiral cucumber salad

Serves 4
2 cucumbers
15ml/1 tbsp salt
90g/3½oz/½ cup granulated
   (white) sugar
175ml/6fl oz/¾ cup dry cider
15ml/1 tbsp cider vinegar
45ml/3 tbsp dill, snipped
Ground black pepper

1 Spiralize the cucumbers using the slicing blade, then cut into shorter lengths. Place in a colander, sprinkling between the layers with the salt. Put the colander over a bowl and leave to drain for 1 hour. Thoroughly rinse the cucumber under cold running water to remove excess salt, then pat dry on kitchen paper.

2 Gently heat the granulated sugar, dry cider and cider vinegar in a pan, stirring until the sugar has dissolved. Remove from the heat and leave to cool.

3 Put the spiralized cucumber in a bowl, pour over the cider mixture and leave to marinate for 2 hours. Drain and sprinkle with snipped dill and ground black pepper to taste. Mix well, transfer to a serving dish and chill until ready to serve.

This Scandinavian fresh pickle is good to serve as an accompaniment with cold poached fresh salmon, smoked fish or sliced meats or cheese. You don't need a chef's knife skills to make this, as a spiralizer will cut cucumber into even thin slices.

Forgo fried onion rings; they are just too high in fat! These crispy-baked spiralized onions with a toasted breadcrumb and cheese topping are an excellent and healthy alternative, and can be made with either white or red onions. Serve as a side dish with grilled meats, chicken and sausages.

Baked spiral shoestring onions

1 Preheat the oven to 200°C/400°F/Gas 6. Spiralize the onions using the medium (3mm/⅛in) spiralizer noodle blade. Snip into shorter lengths about 10cm/4in long. Place on a non-stick baking sheet, season with salt and ground black pepper, then drizzle with sunflower oil. Mix with your hands to coat.

2 Bake for 10 minutes. Meanwhile place the slice of wholemeal or brown bread in a food processor to make fine breadcrumbs and mix with the finely grated cheese.

3 Turn the onions, then sprinkle with the cheese and breadcrumb mixture. Bake for a further 8–10 minutes or until the onions are tender and browned.

 VT

Serves 4
2 large onions
30ml/2 tbsp sunflower oil
1 slice wholemeal (whole-wheat) or
  brown bread
30ml/2 tbsp finely grated vegetarian
  Parmesan cheese
Salt and ground black pepper

DESSERTS & BAKES

From light crisp apple pastries to creamy amaranth pudding and decadent-tasting chocolate torte, this tempting chapter is perfect for anyone with a sweet tooth. Fresh fruit served on its own is the quickest way to end a meal, but with just a little time and a few well-flavoured additions, it can be turned into more special desserts and mid-morning or afternoon treats, as you'll discover here. For those who prefer a savoury bake, you'll find spiralized vegetable muffins and two types of breads, including a soda bread which can be ready to eat in less than an hour.

Coconut, spiralized apple and amaranth pudding

    (if not using Greek yogurt)

Serves 4

250ml/8fl oz/1 cup almond milk

250g/9oz/scant 1½ cups amaranth

Butter, margarine or coconut oil,
   for greasing

3 eating apples, unpeeled and washed

300ml/½ pint/1¼ cups coconut milk,
   plus extra for serving

5ml/1 tsp vanilla extract

2.5ml/½ tsp freshly grated nutmeg

Pinch of salt

Greek (US strained plain) yogurt,
   for serving (optional)

1 Pour the almond milk into a jug or pitcher, add the amaranth and whisk with a fork. Leave to soak for at least 2 hours in the refrigerator or overnight, if preferred.

2 Generously grease an ovenproof dish with butter, margarine or coconut oil. Preheat the oven to 180°C/350°F/Gas 4. Spiralize the apples with the medium (3mm/⅛in) spiralizer noodle blade.

3 Pour the soaked amaranth into the prepared dish. Stir in the coconut milk, vanilla extract, nutmeg and salt.

4 Loosely cover the top of the ovenproof dish with foil. Bake the pudding in the oven for 1½ hours, then remove the foil from the dish and cook for a further 20 minutes or until the amaranth is cooked and the pudding is lightly set and golden-brown.

5 Serve with extra coconut milk or Greek yogurt, if liked.

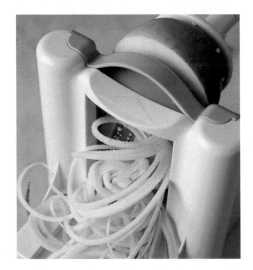

Amaranth grains are as tiny as poppy seeds, but are packed with protein and minerals including iron. Cooking with creamy coconut milk and spiralized eating apples adds natural sweetness, although you may like to serve each portion with a spoonful of agave or maple syrup.

Spiralized slices of pear make an attractive fruity topping for this light sponge which is flavoured with ginger and lime. You can either serve warm as a dessert with thick yogurt or creamy custard, or leave to cool and enjoy as a cake.

Glazed spiralized pear and ginger sponge

1 Grease a loose-bottomed 18cm/7in square tin or pan and line the base with baking parchment. Preheat the oven to 180°C/350°F/Gas 4.

2 Cut halfway through the unpeeled pears from stem end to core, then slice the pears using the spiralizer slicer blade (a horizontal spiralizer is best for this as it will remove the core). Working quickly (before they start to brown), arrange the slices on the bottom of the tin.

3 Put the sugar, oil and lime zest in a bowl and beat them together using a whisk. Add the eggs, one at a time and beat well, then stir in the yogurt. Sift the flour, baking powder and ginger over the egg mixture and fold in until the mixture is smooth. Spoon into the tin over the sliced pears and level the top.

4 Bake for 40–45 minutes, or until the sponge is golden-brown and firm to the touch. Cover with foil towards the end of cooking, if the top starts to brown too much.

5 Leave to cool in the tin for 10 minutes before turning out and carefully removing the lining paper. Cut into 9 squares and serve warm.

Makes 9 portions
3 firm ripe pears
175g/6oz/¾ cup light muscovado (brown) sugar
120ml/4fl oz/½ cup sunflower oil
Finely grated zest of 1 lime
2 eggs
120ml/4fl oz/½ cup plain low-fat yogurt
175g/6oz/1½ cups unbleached plain (all-purpose) flour
7.5ml/1½ tsp baking powder
7.5ml/1½ tsp ground ginger

Cook's tip
Some pear slices will be much wider than others, so arrange them in an attractive pattern.

A spiralizer cuts fantastically thin and even slices of apple which even a professional chef would find challenging. The apples slices are arranged here on layers of filo pastry, brushed with a minimal amount of fat and finished with a sugar glaze to create stunning little fruit tarts. Serve warm with custard or yogurt, if liked.

Apple spiral filo tarts

1 Remove the filo pastry from the refrigerator about 10 minutes before unrolling (this helps stop it from cracking). Line a baking sheet with non-stick baking parchment. Stir the cinnamon into the melted coconut oil or butter.

2 Place a sheet of filo on a board and brush very lightly with the coconut oil or butter, then top with a second sheet of filo. Continue until you have layered up 4 sheets, brushing melted coconut oil or butter very thinly between the layers and over the final layer.

3 Using a small side plate, bowl or saucer as a guide, cut out 2 rounds about 14cm/5½in diameter (a little bigger or smaller is fine). Carefully transfer to the baking sheet. Repeat with the remaining filo pastry sheets to make 4 layered circles of pastry in total.

4 Preheat the oven to 200°C/400°F/Gas 6. Cut halfway through the unpeeled apples from stem end to core, then slice the apples using the spiralizer slicer blade (a horizontal spiralizer is best for this as it will remove the core).

5 Mix together the ground almonds and 10ml/2 tsp of icing sugar. Sprinkle this mixture over the tops of the pastry rounds (this will soak up any juices from the apple slices as they cook and keep the pastry crisp). Arrange the apple slices in concentric circles over the pastry.

6 Using a fine sieve or strainer, dust the tops of the tarts with the remaining 20ml/4 tsp icing sugar (use a little more if there isn't enough to cover all of the tarts). Bake in the oven for 14–15 minutes, (checking towards the end of cooking time as sugar can burn quickly) until the pastry is golden brown and crisp and the apples are tender and lightly caramelized.

 VT DF (and also vegan if using coconut oil not butter)

Makes 4

8 sheets filo pastry, about 30 x 20cm/ 12 x 8in each
1.5ml/¼ tsp ground cinnamon
25g/1oz/2 tbsp coconut oil or unsalted butter, melted
3 medium red-skinned eating apples
30ml/2 tbsp ground almonds
30ml/2 tbsp icing (confectioners') sugar

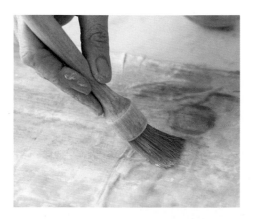

Dark chocolate is good for you! While it's not beneficial to eat large quantities in one go, small amounts provide antioxidants which may reduce blood pressure, and contains the mineral iron. Although it takes a little effort to make this dessert, the resulting silky smooth mousse is worth it. Spooned on top of juicy spiralized pears, they make a great pairing.

Dark chocolate and spiralized pear mousse

  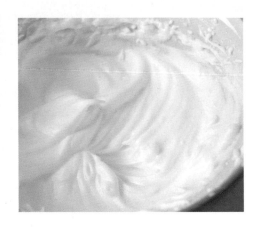

VT **GF**

Serves 4

4 firm ripe red or blush-skinned pears
30ml/2 tbsp orange juice
175g/6oz good-quality dark (semi-sweet) chocolate
10g/¼oz/2 tsp unsalted butter
2 eggs, separated
20ml/1½ tbsp orange liqueur (optional)
40g/1½oz/scant ¼ cup caster (superfine) sugar
Orange zest, to decorate

1 Spiralize the unskinned pears using the medium (3mm/⅛in) spiralizer noodle blade. Put in a bowl, sprinkle over the orange juice and gently mix to coat the noodles (this will stop them turning brown). Divide the noodles between 4 glasses and chill in the refrigerator while making the mousse.

2 Break the chocolate into squares and put in a small pan with 45ml/3 tbsp water. Gently heat, stirring, for 3–5 minutes or until smooth. Remove from the heat and stir in the butter.

3 Return to a low heat and whisk in the egg yolks, one at a time, then whisk for 4 minutes. Turn off the heat, stir in the orange liqueur, if using, then leave until just cool.

4 Put 45ml/3 tbsp water in a small heavy pan, add the sugar and gently heat until dissolved. Boil, without stirring until the syrup is 115°C/240°F on a sugar thermometer, or a few drops in a glass of cold water forms a soft pliable ball.

5 Whisk the egg whites in a clean bowl until stiff, then whisk in the boiling sugar syrup in a thin stream. Continue whisking for 3–4 minutes until the meringue is thick and glossy. Stir a quarter into the chocolate mixture, then fold in the rest. Spoon into the glasses on top of the spiralized pears and chill for at least 1 hour. Decorate with orange zest.

Cook's tip
The eggs in this chocolate mousse are lightly cooked (unlike many mousse recipes which use raw eggs). You should still use really fresh eggs and buy from a reputable source.

Most people won't even guess that this dark decadent-tasting chocolate torte contains finely spiralized raw beetroot. It enriches the colour and adds moistness and texture, making this much lower in fat than most conventional celebration cakes. The cake itself is dairy-free and here it is finished with a light dusting of icing sugar. If you'd like to add a frosting, try the easy ricotta topping suggested here.

Fudgy chocolate and beetroot spiral torte

1 Grease a 20cm/8in tin or pan and line the base with baking parchment. Spiralize the beetroot, with the fine (2mm/¹⁄₁₂in) spiralizer noodle blade. Snip into 2cm/¾in lengths with clean kitchen scissors.

2 Preheat the oven to 160°C/325°F/Gas 3. Break the chocolate into squares and place in a heatproof bowl with the oil over a pan of barely simmering water. Stir occasionally until melted and smooth, then remove the bowl from the heat and set aside to cool for a few minutes.

3 Put the sugar, eggs and vanilla extract in a large bowl and place over the simmering water. Whisk for 4 minutes with an electric whisk until paler in colour and thicker. Add the chocolate mixture and start to fold in, then sift over the flour, 25g/1oz/¼ cup cocoa or cacao powder, bicarbonate of soda and salt, adding the bran left in the sieve or strainer. Add the ground almonds and spiralized beetroot and continue to fold.

4 When the mixture is half folded in, add the almond, coconut or soya milk and continue mixing until evenly blended. Pour into the prepared tin.

5 Bake for 1 hour until the cake is firm, carefully covering the tin with foil after 40 minutes to stop the top over-browning. A fine skewer inserted into the middle of the cake should come out fairly, but not completely, clean as the cake should have a very moist texture.

6 Leave the cake to cool in the tin for 20 minutes, then tip out, top-side down and cool on a wire rack. Dust with icing sugar, then the extra cocoa or cacao powder before serving.

Cook's tip
For a simple frosting, press 250g/9oz/generous 1 cup ricotta cheese through a sieve or strainer into a bowl. Add 5ml/1 tsp vanilla extract and 15ml/1 tbsp sifted icing (confectioners') sugar and beat together until smooth. Spoon the frosting evenly over the top of the cake and use a knife to swirl the frosting, then dust with 5ml/1 tsp cocoa or cacao powder just before serving.

A lovely moist dense chocolate cake which is much healthier than it tastes. Expect the top to crack as it bakes; it's part of the cake's charm

DF **VT**

Makes 12 portions
3 medium beetroot (beets),
　about 300g/11oz
200g/8oz good-quality dark (semi-sweet)
　chocolate
30ml/2 tbsp coconut or sunflower oil
200g/7oz/generous cup light muscovado
　(brown) sugar
3 eggs, at room temperature
10ml/2 tsp vanilla extract
75g/3oz/¾ cup self-raising (self-rising)
　wholemeal (whole-wheat) flour
25g/1oz/¼ cup cocoa or cacao powder,
　plus 5ml/1 tsp for dusting
1.5ml/¼ tsp bicarbonate of soda
　(baking soda)
1.5ml/¼ tsp salt
50g/2oz/½ cup ground almonds
60ml/4 tbsp almond, coconut or soya
　milk, at room temperature
15ml/1 tbsp icing (confectioners') sugar,
　for dusting

This simple recipe containing spiralized courgette is based on soda bread. Don't over-mix and handle gently, or the resulting bake will be heavy. It is best eaten when still slightly warm from the oven.

Spiralized courgette and chilli twisted loaf

VT

Makes 1 medium loaf
350ml/12fl oz/1½ cups buttermilk
15ml/1 tbsp sunflower oil
Pinch of dried chilli flakes (optional)
1 large courgette (zucchini),
    about 250g/9oz
400g/14oz/4 cups unbleached plain
    white (all-purpose) flour, plus extra
    for dusting
5ml/1 tsp salt
10ml/2 tsp bicarbonate of soda
    (baking soda)

1 Put the buttermilk in a jug or pitcher with the oil and chilli flakes, if using. Stir and set aside (the chilli flakes will soften and flavour the buttermilk). Line a baking sheet with baking parchment. Preheat the oven to 220°C/425°F/Gas 7.

2 Spiralize the courgette using the fine (2mm/¹⁄₁₂in) spiralizer noodle blade. Snip the noodles into shorter lengths, about 5cm/2in.

3 Sift the flour, salt and bicarbonate of soda into a bowl, add the courgette noodles and mix into the flour with a round-bladed knife. Make a hollow in the middle, give the buttermilk mixture a quick stir (as the oil will have floated to the top) and add to the hollow. Stir into the dry ingredients until just combined to make a soft, slightly sticky, rough-looking dough.

4 Turn the dough out on to a lightly floured surface and cut into two pieces. Knead each for just a few seconds, then shape into a rope about 25cm/10in long. Lay the ropes side by side, pinch the tops together then gently twist together. Tuck the ends under to neaten and to stop the twist unravelling as it bakes, then transfer to the baking sheet. Dust the top with a little extra flour.

5 Bake for 5 minutes, then lower the temperature to 200°C/400°F/Gas 6 and cook for a further 20–25 minutes or until well-risen and golden-brown. Tap underneath with your knuckles; the loaf will sound hollow when cooked. Transfer to a wire rack to cool.

Spiralized squash and goat's cheese muffins

1 Preheat the oven to 200°C/400°F/Gas 6. Grease a 10-hole muffin tin or pan, or line the holes with paper muffin cases.

2 Spiralize the butternut squash using the fine (2mm/¹⁄₁₂in) spiralizer noodle blade. Snip the noodles into 5cm/2in lengths with clean kitchen scissors.

3 Mix the flour, baking powder, bicarbonate of soda, salt and a few grindings of black pepper in a large bowl. Stir in the goat's cheese, spring onions and 30ml/2 tbsp of the sunflower seeds, then add the spiralized butternut squash, stirring to evenly mix with the dry ingredients.

4 Stir the yogurt, milk, eggs and oil together in a jug or pitcher. Add to the bowl and stir briefly until just combined; the mixture should still be a little lumpy with a few pockets of dry flour.

5 Divide the mixture between the muffin holes or cases, then sprinkle the tops with the remaining 15ml/1 tbsp sunflower seeds. Bake for 20 minutes, or until well-risen and golden. Cool in the tin for 5 minutes, then remove and cool on a wire rack. Serve warm or cold.

Cook's tip
Serve these muffins fresh, preferably while still slightly warm from the oven. They are best eaten within 24 hours of making and should be stored in an airtight container or tin.

Makes 10
225g/8oz piece peeled butternut squash
300g/11oz/3 cups unbleached plain (all-purpose) flour
15ml/1 tbsp baking powder
5ml/1 tsp bicarbonate of soda (baking soda)
2.5ml/½ tsp salt
Ground black pepper
115g/4oz firm goat's cheese, diced
3 spring onions (scallions), trimmed and finely sliced
45ml/3 tbsp sunflower seeds
250ml/8fl oz/1 cup natural (plain) yogurt
15ml/1 tbsp skimmed milk, plus extra for glazing
2 eggs, lightly beaten
30ml/2 tbsp sunflower oil

These savoury muffins make a good alternative to bread to serve with soups and salads. If you have an intolerance to dairy, but can eat goat's milk products, substitute goat's yogurt and milk.

Spiralized sweet potatoes give these small bread rolls an attractive golden colour and rich, slightly sweet flavour. They are baked together in a tin to keep the sides of the individual rolls beautifully soft and the centres moist, but you could arrange them in concentric circles on a baking sheet if you prefer. Simply pull them apart to serve.

Sweet potato spiral bubble bread

1 Spiralize the sweet potatoes using the fine (2mm/1⁄12in) spiralizer noodle blade. Cut the noodles into slightly shorter lengths and put in a pan with the stock or water. Cover with a tight-fitting lid and cook over a low heat for 8 minutes; the sweet potatoes should be just tender and most of the water absorbed.

2 Pour in the milk and add the oil, then re-cover (so that the steam doesn't escape) and leave until tepid. Meanwhile, sift the flours and salt into a bowl and stir in the yeast. Make a hollow in the middle of the dry ingredients.

3 Pour the sweet potato mixture into the hollow and mix to a soft dough. If necessary, add an extra tablespoon or two of milk (this will depend how juicy the sweet potatoes were). Turn out the dough on to a lightly floured surface and knead for 7–8 minutes or until smooth.

4 Put the dough in a lightly oiled bowl, cover with clear film or plastic wrap and leave in a warm place for 1–1½ hours, or until doubled in size. Lightly oil a 25–27cm/10–10½in round tin or pan and line the base with baking parchment.

5 Turn out the dough and knead for 2 minutes to knock out the air bubbles. Divide into 18 equal-sized pieces, then shape each into a ball. Arrange in the tin in two concentric circles with one dough ball in the middle; there should be tiny gaps between each. Cover the tin with clear film and leave the rolls for about 45 minutes or until well-risen.

6 Preheat the oven to 200°C/400°F/Gas 6. Remove the clear film and lightly brush the tops of the rolls with milk. Bake for 20–25 minutes or until well-risen, dark golden and cooked through. Leave in the tin for 5 minutes, then loosen around the sides and turn out on to a wire rack to cool.

VT (vegan and dairy-free if using soya milk)

Makes 18 small rolls
2 medium sweet potatoes,
 about 200g/7oz
75ml/5 tbsp vegetable stock or water
120ml/4fl oz/½ cup skimmed milk or
 soya milk, plus extra for glazing
15ml/1 tbsp sunflower oil
300g/11oz/3 cups strong white bread flour
200g/7oz/2 cups strong wholemeal
 (whole-wheat) bread flour
10ml/2 tsp salt
10ml/2 tsp easy-blend (rapid-rise)
 dried yeast

Nutritional Notes

Basic Vegetable Stock Energy 8kcal/32kJ; Protein 0.4g; Carbohydrate 0.3g, of which sugars 0.1g; Fat 0.5g, of which saturates 0g; Cholesterol 0mg; Calcium 1mg; Fibre 0g; Sodium 39mg.

Simple Vegetable Soup (serves 4) Energy 52kcal/214kJ; Protein 0.6g; Carbohydrate 5.7g, of which sugars 5g; Fat 3.1g, of which saturates 0.5g; Cholesterol 0mg; Calcium 18mg; Fibre 2.1g; Sodium 141mg.

Spiralized Plantain Pancakes (serves 6) Energy 284kcal/1199kJ; Protein 9.2g; Carbohydrate 47.6g, of which sugars 11.2g; Fat 7.6g, of which saturates 1.9g; Cholesterol 81mg; Calcium 115mg; Fibre 3.8g; Sodium 60mg.

Oat and Apple Breakfast Muffins (makes 9) Energy 264kcal/1110kJ; Protein 5.7g; Carbohydrate 38.6g, of which sugars 14.3g; Fat 10.8g, of which saturates 1.6g; Cholesterol 28mg; Calcium 118mg; Fibre 3.1g; Sodium 196mg.

Spiralized Fruit and Seed Breakfast Bars (makes 12) Energy 208kcal/870kJ; Protein 3.9g; Carbohydrate 22.9g, of which sugars 8.4g; Fat 11.8g, of which saturates 5.2g; Cholesterol 13mg; Calcium 35mg; Fibre 3.5g; Sodium 46mg.

Bircher Muesli Spiralizer Style (serves 4) Energy 291kcal/1224kJ; Protein 9.4g; Carbohydrate 39g, of which sugars 14.1g; Fat 11.9g, of which saturates 1.5g; Cholesterol 5mg; Calcium 166mg; Fibre 4.9g; Sodium 67mg.

Chia Porridge with Spiralizer Pear (serves 2) Energy 257kcal/1078kJ; Protein 9g; Carbohydrate 19.3g, of which sugars 17.9g; Fat 15.3g, of which saturates 1.5g; Cholesterol 0mg; Calcium 201mg; Fibre 22.4g; Sodium 537mg.

Eggs Benedict with Spiralized Sweet Potato (serves 4) Energy 312kcal/1305kJ; Protein 15.5g; Carbohydrate 20.7g, of which sugars 7.1g; Fat 19.2g, of which saturates 5.7g; Cholesterol 337mg; Calcium 135mg; Fibre 3g; Sodium 476mg.

Spiralized Squash and Buttermilk Brunch Bread (makes 8 portions) Energy 177kcal/744kJ; Protein 5.1g; Carbohydrate 28.7g, of which sugars 5.8g; Fat 5.1g, of which saturates 3.3g; Cholesterol 30mg; Calcium 89mg; Fibre 1.6g; Sodium 177mg.

Smoked Trout Kedgeree with Spiralized Celeriac (serves 4) Energy 176kcal/725kJ; Protein 5.1g; Carbohydrate 6g, of which sugars 4.5g; Fat 14.6g, of which saturates 10.1g; Cholesterol 162mg; Calcium 101mg; Fibre 10.2g; Sodium 240mg.

Miso Ramen with Spiralized Mooli Noodles (serves 4) Energy 474kcal/1983kJ; Protein 49.7g; Carbohydrate 27.6g, of which sugars 5.3g; Fat 21.6g, of which saturates 1.9g; Cholesterol 231mg; Calcium 386mg; Fibre 0.3g; Sodium 670mg.

Seared Salmon Ramen with Spiralized Courgettes (serves 4) Energy 273kcal/1133kJ; Protein 23.4g; Carbohydrate 4.2g, of which sugars 3.7g; Fat 17.1g, of which saturates 3.1g; Cholesterol 50mg; Calcium 86mg; Fibre 2.6g; Sodium 587mg.

Spiralized Winter Minestrone (serves 6) Energy 123kcal/516kJ; Protein 5.7g; Carbohydrate 19.5g, of which sugars 10.2g; Fat 2.9g, of which saturates 0.4g; Cholesterol 11mg; Calcium 115mg; Fibre 10.7g; Sodium 208mg.

Spiralized Kohlrabi and Apple Soup (serves 4) Energy 113kcal/470kJ; Protein 4.7g; Carbohydrate 16.4g, of which sugars 14.7g; Fat 3.5g, of which saturates 0.3g; Cholesterol 0mg; Calcium 99mg; Fibre 8.9g; Sodium 14mg.

Spiralized Beetroot Broth (serves 4) Energy 109kcal/457kJ; Protein 4g; Carbohydrate 16.2g, of which sugars 14.1g; Fat 3.6g, of which saturates 0.4g; Cholesterol 0mg; Calcium 81mg; Fibre 9.6g; Sodium 178mg.

Paprika Beef and Spiralizer Vegetable Soup (serves 6) Energy 257kcal/1080kJ; Protein 19.8g; Carbohydrate 25.6g, of which sugars 9.1g; Fat 9.1g, of which saturates 2g; Cholesterol 73mg; Calcium 101mg; Fibre 4.4g; Sodium 240mg.

Roasted Courgette Soup with Minted Tzatziki (serves 4) Energy 222kcal/919kJ; Protein 10.5g; Carbohydrate 14.9g, of which sugars 12.9g; Fat 13.7g, of which saturates 5.4g; Cholesterol 10mg; Calcium 191mg; Fibre 8.1g; Sodium 51mg.

Chilled Spiralizer Gazpacho (serves 6) Energy 153kcal/640kJ; Protein 3.3g; Carbohydrate 17.4g, of which sugars 7.1g; Fat 8.3g, of which saturates 1.3g; Cholesterol 0mg; Calcium 46mg; Fibre 3.2g; Sodium 124mg.

Raw Pad Thai with Spiralized Noodles (serves 4) Energy 123kcal/510kJ; Protein 4.9g; Carbohydrate 11.7g, of which sugars 7.9g; Fat 6.5g, of which saturates 1g; Cholesterol 0mg; Calcium 109mg; Fibre 4.9g; Sodium 1360mg.

Salad of Roasted Spiralized Beetroot (serves 4) Energy 343kcal/1423kJ; Protein 8.5g; Carbohydrate 14.7g, of which sugars 13.4g; Fat 29.7g, of which saturates 3.6g; Cholesterol 0mg; Calcium 145mg; Fibre 6.1g; Sodium 164mg.

Creamy Spiralized Root Vegetable Salad (serves 4) Energy 135kcal/564kJ; Protein 2.8g; Carbohydrate 15.4g, of which sugars 7.1g; Fat 7.3g, of which saturates 1.1g; Cholesterol 11mg; Calcium 86mg; Fibre 7.5g; Sodium 158mg.

Spiralized Mooli Salad with Wasabi Dressing (serves 4) Energy 74kcal/305kJ; Protein 1.4g; Carbohydrate 4.5g, of which sugars 4.5g; Fat 5.7g, of which saturates 0.8g; Cholesterol 0mg; Calcium 53mg; Fibre 0g; Sodium 43mg.

Fennel Carpacio (serves 4) Energy 120kcal/495kJ; Protein 3.5g; Carbohydrate 3.4g, of which sugars 3.3g; Fat 10.4g, of which saturates 2.3g; Cholesterol 6mg; Calcium 95mg; Fibre 4g; Sodium 62mg.

Sprouted Salad with Tofu Dressing (serves 4) Energy 262kcal/1093kJ; Protein 17.8g; Carbohydrate 20.3g, of which sugars 12.4g; Fat 13.6g, of which saturates 1g; Cholesterol 0mg; Calcium 171mg; Fibre 4.2g; Sodium 22mg.

Spiralized Indonesian Vegetable Salad (serves 4) Energy 190kcal/790kJ; Protein 10.5g; Carbohydrate 14.5g, of which sugars 6.4g; Fat 10.3g, of which saturates 2.5g; Cholesterol 248mg; Calcium 109mg; Fibre 5g; Sodium 385mg.

Quinoa Salad with Spiralized Cucumber and Mooli (serves 4) Energy 426kcal/1769kJ; Protein 17.4g; Carbohydrate 14.8g, of which sugars 4.8g; Fat 33.4g, of which saturates 10.8g; Cholesterol 36mg; Calcium 293mg; Fibre 0.7g; Sodium 406mg.

Chayote and Avocado Salad with Green Chilli (serves 4) Energy 229kcal/944kJ; Protein 3.1g; Carbohydrate 3.1g, of which sugars 2g; Fat 22.8g, of which saturates 4.1g; Cholesterol 0mg; Calcium 37mg; Fibre 4.3g; Sodium 7mg.

Ratatouille Salad (serves 6) Energy 119kcal/492kJ; Protein 3.1g; Carbohydrate 8.4g, of which sugars 7.5g; Fat 8.3g, of which saturates 1.3g; Cholesterol 0mg; Calcium 40mg; Fibre 5.1g; Sodium 8mg.

Beef and Mushrooms with Spiralized Rosti (serves 4) Energy 621kcal/2590kJ; Protein 32.5g; Carbohydrate 45.6g, of which sugars 16.8g; Fat 35.4g, of which saturates 14g; Cholesterol 136mg; Calcium 171mg; Fibre 13g; Sodium 298mg.

Slow Braised Beef with Spiralized Beetroot (serves 4) Energy 346kcal/1451kJ; Protein 42.3g; Carbohydrate 13.9g, of which sugars 11.1g; Fat 13.9g, of which saturates 3.8g; Cholesterol 102mg; Calcium 83mg; Fibre 4.3g; Sodium 444mg.

Beef and Courgetti Lasagne (serves 6) Energy 264kcal/1103kJ; Protein 24g; Carbohydrate 15.2g, of which sugars 9.5g; Fat 12.3g, of which saturates 5.2g; Cholesterol 47mg; Calcium 190mg; Fibre 4.2g; Sodium 150mg.

Teryaki Beef Spiralized Stir-Fry (serves 4) Energy 235kcal/977kJ; Protein 23.4g; Carbohydrate 8.6g, of which sugars 8g; Fat 10.1g, of which saturates 2.4g; Cholesterol 51mg; Calcium 71mg; Fibre 3.8g; Sodium 1149mg.

Venison Medallions on a Bed of Spiralized Beetroot and Sweet Potato (serves 4) Energy 290kcal/1227kJ; Protein 31.2g; Carbohydrate 27.3g, of which sugars 15.5g; Fat 6.9g, of which saturates 1.7g; Cholesterol 63mg; Calcium 60mg; Fibre 6g; Sodium 170mg.

Five Spice Pork and Spiralized Apple Patties (serves 4) Energy 382kcal/1596kJ; Protein 27.2g; Carbohydrate 20g, of which sugars 7.9g; Fat 22.1g, of which saturates 5.6g; Cholesterol 132mg; Calcium 46mg; Fibre 1.8g; Sodium 111mg.

Sweet Seared Pork with Spiralized Red Cabbage (serves 4) Energy 557kcal/2315kJ; Protein 32.4g; Carbohydrate 16.7g, of which sugars 14.4g; Fat 37.8g, of which saturates 12g; Cholesterol 110mg; Calcium 112mg; Fibre 5.4g; Sodium 514mg.

Red-Roasted Pork with Spiralized Courgette and Carrot Noodles (serves 4) Energy 306kcal/1278kJ; Protein 28.8g; Carbohydrate 8.7g, of which sugars 8.2g; Fat 16.6g, of which saturates 3.7g; Cholesterol 71mg; Calcium 91mg; Fibre 4.2g; Sodium 913mg.

Spiced Lamb with Lentils and Spiralized Butternut Squash (serves 4) Energy 408kcal/1718kJ; Protein 35.4g; Carbohydrate 33.5g, of which sugars 8.5g; Fat 15.7g, of which saturates 4.7g; Cholesterol 83mg; Calcium 111mg; Fibre 8.5g; Sodium 97mg.

Flash Fry Lamb and Spiralized Salad Pittas (serves 4) Energy 420kcal/1762kJ; Protein 28.8g; Carbohydrate 37.5g, of which sugars 5.3g; Fat 18.2g, of which saturates 5.2g; Cholesterol 83mg; Calcium 114mg; Fibre 2.9g; Sodium 353mg.

Courgette Carbonara (serves 4) Energy 283kcal/1170kJ; Protein 20.2g; Carbohydrate 4.6g, of which sugars 4.4g; Fat 20.4g, of which saturates 7.5g; Cholesterol 347mg; Calcium 233mg; Fibre 3g; Sodium 510mg.

Lemon Chicken with Courgetti (serves 4) Energy 331kcal/1381kJ; Protein 36.5g; Carbohydrate 10.9g, of which sugars 9.1g; Fat 15.9g, of which saturates 2.5g; Cholesterol 88mg; Calcium 121mg; Fibre 4.8g; Sodium 273mg.

Chicken Layered with Spiralized Salad (serves 4) Energy 314kcal/1314kJ; Protein 36.4g; Carbohydrate 17.5g, of which sugars 17g; Fat 11.3g, of which saturates 1.8g; Cholesterol 88mg; Calcium 126mg; Fibre 7.6g; Sodium 142mg.

Chicken and Almond Pilaf with Spiralized Rice (serves 4) Energy 403kcal/1692kJ; Protein 27.5g; Carbohydrate 36.1g, of which sugars 16.8g; Fat 17.6g, of which saturates 1.9g; Cholesterol 44mg; Calcium 226mg; Fibre 12.1g; Sodium 315mg.

Sautéed Chicken Livers with Sage and Onion on Spiralized Potato Galettes (serves 4) Energy 295kcal/1234kJ; Protein 20.4g; Carbohydrate 23.2g, of which sugars 5g; Fat 14g, of which saturates 2.3g; Cholesterol 417mg; Calcium 55mg; Fibre 3g; Sodium 100mg.

Turkey Enchiladas with Spiralized Vegetables (serves 4) Energy 670kcal/2818kJ; Protein 30.3g; Carbohydrate 90.1g, of which sugars 11.8g; Fat 24.8g, of which saturates 13.2g; Cholesterol 91mg; Calcium 407mg; Fibre 7.9g; Sodium 556mg.

Aromatic Duck with Spiralized Potato and Beetroot Ribbons (serves 4) Energy 354kcal/1485kJ; Protein 25.9g; Carbohydrate 35.2g, of which sugars 17.9g; Fat 12.7g, of which saturates 2.8g; Cholesterol 139mg; Calcium 90mg; Fibre 7.2g; Sodium 353mg.

Cod with Chorizo and Spiralized Vegetable Lentils (serves 4) Energy 362kcal/1521kJ; Protein 43.2g; Carbohydrate 27.6g, of which sugars 5.6g; Fat 9.4g, of which saturates 2.5g; Cholesterol 69mg; Calcium 78mg; Fibre 7.5g; Sodium 214mg.

Grilled Seabass with Spiralized Fennel Potato Rosti (serves 4) Energy 322kcal/1351kJ; Protein 33.9g; Carbohydrate 21.9g, of which sugars 3.3g; Fat 11.5g, of which saturates 2g; Cholesterol 219mg; Calcium 235mg; Fibre 4.9g; Sodium 149mg.

Smoked Trout and Spiralized Carrot Roulade (serves 6) Energy 237kcal/982kJ; Protein 10.8g; Carbohydrate 7.6g, of which sugars 4.2g; Fat 18.3g, of which saturates 10.4g; Cholesterol 161mg; Calcium 85mg; Fibre 1.5g; Sodium 461mg.

Spiralized Seafood Laksa (serves 4) Energy 217kcal/915kJ; Protein 33.5g; Carbohydrate 11.6g, of which sugars 10.6g; Fat 4.4g, of which saturates 0.9g; Cholesterol 211mg; Calcium 151mg; Fibre 2.3g; Sodium 890mg.

Salmon and Spiralized Potato Cakes with Celeriac (Serves 2) Energy 722kcal/3003kJ; Protein 33.4g; Carbohydrate 42.5g, of which sugars 11.8g; Fat 47.4g, of which saturates 14.1g; Cholesterol 273mg; Calcium 203mg; Fibre 13.4g; Sodium 398mg.

Tuna Spiralizer Niçoise (Serves 4) Energy 300kcal/1255kJ; Protein 38g; Carbohydrate 4.3g, of which sugars 4.2g; Fat 14.6g, of which saturates 3g; Cholesterol 42mg; Calcium 76mg; Fibre 5.1g; Sodium 424mg.

Courgetti Alla Puttanesca (serves 4) Energy 329kcal/1354kJ; Protein 12.9g; Carbohydrate 10.9g, of which sugars 10.3g; Fat 26g, of which saturates 4g; Cholesterol 8mg; Calcium 189mg; Fibre 7.4g; Sodium 505mg.

Crispy Prawn Spring Rolls (serves 4) Energy 201kcal/843kJ; Protein 10g; Carbohydrate 24.2g, of which sugars 4.4g; Fat 7.3g, of which saturates 1.4g; Cholesterol 56mg; Calcium 93mg; Fibre 3.4g; Sodium 603mg.

Warm Courgette Rice and Pepper Noodle Salad with Seafood (serves 4) Energy 238kcal/987kJ; Protein 17.2g; Carbohydrate 12.9g, of which sugars 9.8g; Fat 13.2g, of which saturates 2.1g; Cholesterol 41mg; Calcium 110mg; Fibre 6.1g; Sodium 339mg.

Coodles with Creamy Avocado Sauce (Serves 4) Energy 233kcal/958kJ; Protein 5.9g; Carbohydrate 5.9g, of which sugars 4.7g; Fat 20.6g, of which saturates 4g; Cholesterol 0mg; Calcium 71mg; Fibre 6.3g; Sodium 7mg.

Courgette Ribbons with Arrabbiata Sauce (serves 4) Energy 152kcal/632kJ; Protein 6.4g; Carbohydrate 10.6g, of which sugars 10.2g; Fat 9.8g, of which saturates 1.5g; Cholesterol 0mg; Calcium 97mg; Fibre 5.3g; Sodium 52mg.

Thai Spiralized Vegetable Omelette (serves 4) Energy 77kcal/325kJ; Protein 3.2g; Carbohydrate 11.1g, of which sugars 6.2g; Fat 2.5g, of which saturates 0.6g; Cholesterol 46mg; Calcium 54mg; Fibre 3g; Sodium 578mg.

Courgetti Genovese (serves 4) Energy 372kcal/1538kJ; Protein 8.7g; Carbohydrate 14g, of which sugars 5.8g; Fat 31.5g, of which saturates 4.9g; Cholesterol 22mg; Calcium 149mg; Fibre 4g; Sodium 66mg.

Summer Frittata with Spiralized Salsa (serves 4) Energy 391kcal/1626kJ; Protein 22g; Carbohydrate 21.3g, of which sugars 12.5g; Fat 24.6g, of which saturates 8g; Cholesterol 480mg; Calcium 191mg; Fibre 6.7g; Sodium 320mg.

Spicy Spiralized Plantain Rice and Beans (serves 4) Energy 378kcal/1607kJ; Protein 9.2g; Carbohydrate 81.2g, of which sugars 19.4g; Fat 4.2g, of which saturates 0.8g; Cholesterol 0mg; Calcium 69mg; Fibre 8g; Sodium 83mg.

Butternut Squash and Broccoli Noodles (serves 4) Energy 310kcal/1291kJ; Protein 12.7g; Carbohydrate 15g, of which sugars 8.8g; Fat 22.6g, of which saturates 9.5g; Cholesterol 36mg; Calcium 267mg; Fibre 4.8g; Sodium 431mg.

Meditteranean Spiral Vegetable and Polenta Pizza (serves 4) Energy 468kcal/1950kJ; Protein 16.3g; Carbohydrate 63.2g, of which sugars 6.4g; Fat 16.2g, of which saturates 5.4g; Cholesterol 18mg; Calcium 177mg; Fibre 5.7g; Sodium 479mg.

Glazed Spiralized Swede with Couscous (serves 4) Energy 217kcal/904kJ; Protein 4.4g; Carbohydrate 37.1g, of which sugars 8.4g; Fat 6.6g, of which saturates 0.8g; Cholesterol 0mg; Calcium 117mg; Fibre 4.5g; Sodium 42mg.

Spiralized Cheese, Onoin and Potato Bake (Serves 6) Energy 364kcal/1527kJ; Protein 15.7g; Carbohydrate 40.9g, of which sugars 3.8g; Fat 16.4g, of which saturates 6.3g; Cholesterol 121mg; Calcium 248mg; Fibre 5.6g; Sodium 267mg.

Spiralized Falafels and Sesame Pitta Fingers (serves 4) Energy 429kcal/1795kJ; Protein 14.2g; Carbohydrate 38.9g, of which sugars 6g; Fat 25.2g, of which saturates 5.7g; Cholesterol 6mg; Calcium 235mg; Fibre 5.3g; Sodium 711mg.

Spiralized Pepper and Tomato Ragoût (serves 4) Energy 190kcal/791kJ; Protein 10.2g; Carbohydrate 14.8g, of which sugars 12.8g; Fat 10.4g, of which saturates 2.5g; Cholesterol 231mg; Calcium 82mg; Fibre 5.1g; Sodium 101mg.

Spiralized Mooli Noodles with Mushrooms (serves 4) Energy 99kcal/413kJ; Protein 5g; Carbohydrate 6.4g, of which sugars 5.6g; Fat 6.1g, of which saturates 1.1g; Cholesterol 58mg; Calcium 69mg; Fibre 2.3g; Sodium 65mg.

Spiralized Vegetable Tempura (serves 4) Energy 482kcal/2017kJ; Protein 26.3g; Carbohydrate 45.7g, of which sugars 8.4g; Fat 22.7g, of which saturates 2g; Cholesterol 0mg; Calcium 244mg; Fibre 4.9g; Sodium 1093mg.

Spiralized Curly Fries (serves 4) Energy 128kcal/539kJ; Protein 1.9g; Carbohydrate 18.1g, of which sugars 1.5g; Fat 5.8g, of which saturates 0.9g; Cholesterol 37mg; Calcium 7mg; Fibre 1.5g; Sodium 258mg.

Spiralized Potato Kugel (serves 4) Energy 235kcal/986kJ; Protein 8.7g; Carbohydrate 26.9g, of which sugars 3.7g; Fat 11.1g, of which saturates 2.2g; Cholesterol 210mg; Calcium 52mg; Fibre 2.5g; Sodium 77mg.

Spiralized Potato Latkes (serves 4) Energy 224kcal/939kJ; Protein 7.8g; Carbohydrate 26.9g, of which sugars 3.7g; Fat 10.2g, of which saturates 2g; Cholesterol 182mg; Calcium 48mg; Fibre 2.5g; Sodium 66mg.

Spiralized Mixed Pepper Piperade (serves 2) Energy 413kcal/1718kJ; Protein 19.5g; Carbohydrate 26.6g, of which sugars 24.1g; Fat 26.1g, of which saturates 5.8g; Cholesterol 462mg; Calcium 119mg; Fibre 8.8g; Sodium 196mg.

Marinated Spiral Cucumber Salad (serves 4) Energy 117kcal/497kJ; Protein 1.2g; Carbohydrate 26.3g, of which sugars 26.2g; Fat 0.2g, of which saturates 0g; Cholesterol 0mg; Calcium 66mg; Fibre 1.2g; Sodium 10mg.

Baked Spiral Shoestring Onions (serves 4) Energy 142kcal/590kJ; Protein 4.9g; Carbohydrate 13.1g, of which sugars 7.3g; Fat 8.2g, of which saturates 2.2g; Cholesterol 7mg; Calcium 116mg; Fibre 2.9g; Sodium 97mg.

Coconut, Spiralized Apple & Amaranth Pudding (serves 4) Energy 126kcal/531kJ; Protein 3.1g; Carbohydrate 26.4g, of which sugars 13.8g; Fat 1.8g, of which saturates 0.2g; Cholesterol 0mg; Calcium 25mg; Fibre 1.8g; Sodium 130mg.

Glazed Spiralized Pear and Ginger Sponge (makes 9) Energy 274kcal/1153kJ; Protein 4.5g; Carbohydrate 42.2g, of which sugars 26.8g; Fat 10.8g, of which saturates 1.6g; Cholesterol 52mg; Calcium 78mg; Fibre 2.3g; Sodium 129mg.

Apple Spiral FiloTarts (serves 4) Energy 245kcal/1031kJ; Protein 4.2g; Carbohydrate 36.7g, of which sugars 17.3g; Fat 10.1g, of which saturates 5.2g; Cholesterol 0mg; Calcium 56mg; Fibre 2.8g; Sodium 5mg.

Dark Chocolate & Spiralized Pear Mousse (serves 4) Energy 351kcal/1474kJ; Protein 3.4g; Carbohydrate 53.9g, of which sugars 53.5g; Fat 14.9g, of which saturates 8.8g; Cholesterol 27mg; Calcium 38mg; Fibre 5.9g; Sodium 16mg.

Fudgy Chocolate and Beetroot Spiral Torte (serves 12) Energy 258kcal/1085kJ; Protein 5.1g; Carbohydrate 35.3g, of which sugars 30g; Fat 11.8g, of which saturates 4g; Cholesterol 59mg; Calcium 59mg; Fibre 1.8g; Sodium 135mg.

Spiralized Courgette and Chilli Twisted Loaf (makes 1) Energy 1637kcal/6941kJ; Protein 54g; Carbohydrate 332.8g, of which sugars 27.8g; Fat 18.9g, of which saturates 3.4g; Cholesterol 7mg; Calcium 1043mg; Fibre 19.5g; Sodium 4914mg.

Spiralized Squash and Goat's Cheese Muffins (serves 10) Energy 229kcal/964kJ; Protein 9.3g; Carbohydrate 28.7g, of which sugars 3.7g; Fat 9.4g, of which saturates 3.2g; Cholesterol 57mg; Calcium 140mg; Fibre 2.1g; Sodium 419mg.

Sweet Potato Spiral Bubble Bread (makes 18) Energy 110kcal/465kJ; Protein 3.3g; Carbohydrate 22.7g, of which sugars 1.4g; Fat 1.2g, of which saturates 0.2g; Cholesterol 0mg; Calcium 38mg; Fibre 2.4g; Sodium 227mg.

Index

Acknowledgements

This edition is published by Lorenz Books, an imprint of Anness Publishing Ltd, 108 Great Russell Street, London WC1B 3NA; info@anness.com

www.lorenzbooks.com;
www.annesspublishing.com;
twitter: @Anness_Books

If you like the images in this book and would like to investigate using them for publishing, promotions or advertising, please visit our website www.practicalpictures.com for more information.

© Anness Publishing Ltd 2015

A CIP catalogue record for this book is available from the British Library.

Publisher: Joanna Lorenz
Photography and styling: Nicki Dowey
Food stylist: Jayne Cross
Designer: Adelle Mahoney
Editorial: Sarah Lumby

With many thanks for their help in supplying spiralizers: Lakeland (www.lakeland.co.uk), Cuisique (www.cuisique.co.uk) and UK Juicers (www.ukjuicers.com).

PUBLISHER'S NOTE
Although the advice and information in this book are believed to be accurate and true at the time of going to press, neither the authors nor the publisher can accept any legal responsibility or liability for any errors or omissions that may have been made nor for any inaccuracies nor for any loss, harm or injury that comes about from following instructions or advice in this book.

COOK'S NOTES
Bracketed terms are intended for American readers.
For all recipes, quantities are given in both metric and imperial measures and, where appropriate, in standard cups and spoons. Follow one set of measures, but not a mixture, because they are not interchangeable.
Standard spoon and cup measures are level. 1 tsp = 5ml, 1 tbsp = 15ml, 1 cup = 250ml/8fl oz.
Australian standard tablespoons are 20ml. Australian readers should use 3 tsp in place of 1 tbsp for measuring small quantities.
American pints are 16fl oz/2 cups. American readers should use 20fl oz/2.5 cups in place of 1 pint when measuring liquids.
Electric oven temperatures in this book are for conventional ovens. When using a fan oven, the temperature will probably need to be reduced by about 10–20°C/20–40°F. Since ovens vary, you should check with your manufacturer's instruction book for guidance.
Medium (US large) eggs are used unless otherwise stated.